# The SENCO Essential Manual

# The SENCO Essential Manual

Sue Soan

McGraw Hill Education
Open University Press

Open University Press
McGraw-Hill Education
8th Floor
338 Euston Road
London
NW1 3BH

email: enquiries@openup.co.uk
world wide web: www.mheducation.co.uk

and Two Penn Plaza, New York, NY 10121-2289, USA

First published 2017



A catalogue record of this book is available from the British Library

ISBN-13: 978-0-33-526138-3
ISBN-10: 0-33-526138-8
eISBN: 978-0-33-526139-0

*Library of Congress Cataloging-in-Publication Data*
CIP data applied for

Typeset by Transforma Pvt. Ltd., Chennai, India



Printed and bound by CPI Group (UK) Ltd, Croydon, CR0 4YY

# Praise for this book

***"The SENCO Essential Manual provides comprehensive practical guidance on key aspects of the SENCO role. The close alignment of its content with Learning Outcomes for the National Award for Special Educational Needs Co-ordination make it especially useful for practitioners working to achieve this qualification. Key strengths include the engaging style of writing and an accessible format that combines presentation of essential information, discussion of enduring and emerging issues and questions and suggestions for practice. For the busy SENCO this book is likely to represent a very welcome 'one-stop' guide to support the development of their own and their setting's practice."***

*Dr Simon Ellis, Senior Lecturer, Faculty of Education, Canterbury Christ Church University, UK*

***"The SENCo Essential Manual is an invaluable resource for aspiring and newly appointed SENCos, as well as for those with experience who wish to update their knowledge in response to recent policy developments. The manual clearly and comprehensively guides SENCos through the multifaceted responsibilities of the role, in addition to addressing the key areas that SENCos need to understand in order to execute their operational and strategic responsibilities. A particular strength of this guide is its use of practice-based questions and suggestions to encourage SENCos' setting-specific reflection on the various topics."***

*Louise Hamilton, Senior Lecturer, Bath Spa University, UK*

***"This book is an essential manual for all SENCOs; highly readable, up-to-date and informative. The text clearly links policy to the specifics of excellent day-to-day practice. Covering a comprehensive range of topics, this book will support professionals to achieve the ultimate goal, good outcomes for children and young people."***

*Dr Geraldene Codina, Senior Lecturer, Institute of Education, University of Derby, UK*

This book is dedicated to every SENCO. Thank you for your commitment to and belief in our children. You do make a difference.

# Contents

# List of figures

# List of tables

# List of case studies

# Foreword

I am delighted to write this foreword to *The SENCO Essential Manual*. Sue Soan is very well placed write about the role of the SENCO having worked as a SENCO for many years and supported many teachers, as a university-based teacher educator, to gain the National Award for SEN Co-ordination since its introduction in England in 2009. More importantly than being well qualified to share such advice on the role of SENCO, particularly for those new to the role, Sue clearly recognises the importance of providing guidance that is both practical and educationally effective but also manageable for teacher colleagues whose professional lives are extremely demanding. She is 'up front' about wanting to support SENCOs in getting the essentials right rather than trying to exemplify a special educational needs co-ordination ideal, or theorize about the role without grounding in it the real world of schools and related education settings.

*The SENCO Essential Manual* is succinct but really does give SENCOs an appropriate amount of advice about how to the carry out day-to-day, strategic and leadership aspects of the role in an informed and manageable way. Furthermore, it is a resource that will help teachers undertaking the National Award for SEN Co-ordination to achieve all of its specified learning outcomes.*

Three key principles underpin the book's approach to SEN co-ordination. First, the importance of **adopting a whole school/setting approach** to identifying, assessing and meeting the needs of children and young is emphasised throughout. Second, **developing personalized learning contexts** for all children and young people is considered imperative. Third, **collaboration between a range of partners** - including children, young people and their families – is seen as key to the achievement of good quality person-centred learning outcomes. These principles, based on good evidence, inform all of the practical advice that the book provides and the case study examples it includes.

In recommending *The SENCO Essential Manual* I think it worth noting that the book will be of value to a range of special educational needs professionals, as well as those working closely with them. Aspiring SENCOs, those just embarking on a SENCO career, those starting a course of study leading to the National Award for SEN Co-ordination qualification, and more experienced SENCO practitioners wanting a 'knowledge and good practice' update, will find it to be both a comprehensive and accessible 'go-to' resource. Headteachers and governing bodies/proprietors will also find that it provides clear guidance on how the role of a SENCO should be carried out, and will help them to support the development of

---

*National College for Teaching and Leadership (2014) *National Award for SEN Co-ordination: Learning Outcomes*. https://www.gov.uk/government/publications/national-award-for-sen-co-ordination-learning-outcomes

SEN provision that they are responsible for. It might also be used to help them recruit a good SENCO in the future!

Christopher Robertson

Honorary Lecturer, University of Birmingham School of Education, and Programme Lead for the SEN Co-ordination programmes (including the National Award for SEN Co-ordination) from 2001–2015.

Chair, SENCO Forum Advisory Group (national e-discussion community)

# Preface

Why another SENCO book? I have been a tutor at a university on the National Award for Special Educational Needs Co-ordination since its inception and have therefore worked with a large number of both new and experienced SENCOs before, during and since the implementation of the current SEND Code of Practice (DfE and DoH, 2015). I have also been a SENCO myself between 1994 and 2003 and then again in 2013, in primary, secondary and special schools and have experienced the ever-changing landscape within which the SENCO has to manoeuvre. What SENCOs have constantly asked for across the years (including myself) is a manual stating what can often seem to be the obvious things, but which can help them avoid wasting time and energy, while still fulfilling their roles and responsibilities. I hope this manual fills this gap.

SENCOs have always needed to be resilient, passionate about learning for all, knowledgeable about atypical learning development and excellent communicators, but during the past decade, leadership and being a strategist have also been added to the list of required expertise. Recognizing the significance and high-level demands of the role, the UK government introduced the National Award as a Master Level qualification (Postgraduate Certificate) as a requirement all new SENCOs have to complete within three years of taking on the role in England. Essential theoretical, reflective thinking and critical understanding are undoubtedly achieved through this Award, but there is still a need for SENCOs to have a manual which helps them link policy to practice on a daily basis. While this manual will positively encourage criticality, research and reflection, its main purpose is to provide a SENCO with the 'how to' and offer practical ideas.

# Introduction

All SENCOs and especially those new to the role need to have a practical reference resource, their 'go-to document', that explicitly informs them what they must do to meet national statutory requirements, and when and how these should be implemented. *The SENCO Essential Manual* provides both this clarity and the practical ideas to enable positive outcomes for all pupils in all educational establishments. Indeed, the manual will be relevant not only to SENCOs, but to all teachers and other educators, including head teachers and other statutory professionals, such as social workers and health colleagues. *The SENCO Essential Manual* also considers issues and provides ideas for all schools and settings across all phases and designations.

Additionally, the manual briefly provides an overview of why a SENCO is now expected by the government in England to be a strategic leader, and how this needs to inform and direct their daily practice and professional knowledge. Personalization, inclusion and diversity are discussed and related to the values and ethos of educational establishments, enabling SENCOs to see how their role can be instrumental in determining the direction and success of their development.

The information in this manual is presented in a manner that supports the way SENCOs need to work in their busy and complex educational environments. Practice questions, strategies, tables and ideas are included and presented in a manner which fully supports electronic copying.

## 0.1 Overview of the book

*The SENCO Essential Manual* contains seven chapters. While great attention has been paid to ensuring the Accredited SENCO Learning Outcomes are discussed, the chapters focus primarily on the roles and responsibilities of a SENCO, as directed by the SEND Code of Practice (DfE and DoH, 2015). Chapters 1–6 concentrate on specific broad responsibilities for SENCOs, while Chapter 7 supports SENCOs in the development of a three-year strategic plan which meets both the individual and local needs of their educational institution and also national expectations. At the end of each chapter there is a section 'What does this mean for the SENCO?' and the final part is entitled: 'Direct links to the SEND Code of Practice (DfE and DoH, 2015)'. Here actual guidance detailed in the SEND Code of Practice (DfE and DoH, 2015) is provided to illustrate areas discussed in the chapter, covering specific aspects for SENCOs (or the SEN named person) working in early years' provisions, schools and colleges. There is a list of resources in some chapters and also a full reference list at the rear of the book.

## Chapter 1 The development of the SENCO role

In this first chapter, SEN legislation and policy are used to describe the role of the SENCO as a strategic leader. This view of the role provides you with knowledge of current legislation and national guidance documents and information about how this influences and directs practice. Personalization, inclusion and diversity are discussed in terms of how SENCOs are now expected to use their leadership and strategic role to embed and enhance personalization pedagogical practice in their workplace. In the final section of this chapter the roles and responsibilities of a SENCO are explained. To put these into perspective a brief look at how these have changed from the original SEN Code of Practice (DfE, 1994) to the current Code (DfE and DoH, 2015), linking them to the policy and agendas of the time is presented. In this way you can directly see how expectations of the role have evolved to its current position working within the framework of the present SEND Code of Practice (DfE and DoH, 2015).

## Chapter 2 Leading, developing and supporting colleagues

For many SENCOs, this will be your first opportunity to engage with what leadership actually is. First, the differences and similarities between being a manager and a leader are explained. Factors which will help a SENCO employ the right staff for the right roles are then explored. This chapter also explains what quality first teaching with regards to SEN looks like in a class, enabling the facilitation of effective learning for the majority of children or young people. In this discussion you are given guidance on how to help staff develop their skills and knowledge of atypical learning development within a collaborative environment. For many SENCOs, undertaking performance management for teaching colleagues and other staff such as teaching assistants and learning mentors requires new skills and so this is discussed with a particular focus on the promotion of staff well-being.

## Chapter 3 The SENCO and whole school development

This chapter commences by explaining how the SENCO needs to ensure that SEN is enshrined within all aspects of whole school planning and action and is not just considered as an 'add-on' or in a separate manner. This is first of all explored and evidenced by looking at the various duties and requirements of a SENCO, such as the SEN Information Report and SEN Policy. The chapter then illustrates how this way of thinking can also apply to financial and business development decisions within settings, and considers the role of the SENCO in helping to ensure these are in the interest of all children or young people. It includes information about budgeting and also costing of time and equipment, especially with regards to Education, Health and Care (EHC) plans. The current focus on progress and outcomes rather than on 'provision' is considered next to show how it could impact on and influence how budgets are managed. Another aspect of this for the SENCO to consider is how SEN initial or continuing professional development for all staff is provided to meet your establishment's requirements. It is at this point that you are introduced to Action Research and Evidence-based Practice as tools to inform practice and whole school development. An example will be presented here, detailing how a SENCO can undertake research to support not only better practice for children or young people, but better financial decisions as well.

### Chapter 4 The co-ordination of provision

Chapter 4 commences with the identification of the SEN areas of need as detailed in the SEND Code of Practice (DfE and DoH, 2015). Carrying forward discussions from Chapters 2 and 3 about the importance of impact and outcomes and how this needs to influence business and financial decisions, the focus on individual children's or young people's special educational needs will be explored. This leads on to how SENCOs need to organize and manage the identification and assessment of need within their own educational setting within the national framework of SEN support (the Graduated Approach) and Education, Health and Care (EHC) plans. At the end of this chapter the role of successful transitions and their heightened significance are included, providing a holistic view of why they can make so much difference to progress and well-being for all children and young people, but particularly those with a special educational need.

### Chapter 5 The personalized learning environment

The importance of the learning environment for children and young people with special educational needs is frequently underestimated. Hence Chapter 5 adds breadth and depth to the SENCO discussions about whole school development through an exploration of this field of enquiry. It enables SENCOs to expand their understanding and knowledge about how to help create and develop an inclusive environment. The barriers and strengths of specific physical environments will be considered from a SEN, disability, behavioural and business point of view, and suggestions are made to enhance practice for all. Once the physical aspects of a learning environment have been discussed, factors connected to making educational settings safe environments, including safeguarding and child protection, are also examined in light of the various national guidance documents and legislation.

### Chapter 6 Working together

Chapter 6, I believe, is the most challenging chapter for some SENCOs because it challenges you to review and reflect on whole school processes and systems and to determine what needs to be introduced or enhanced further so that all children and young people are participants in moving the school forward. Likewise, this way of thinking needs to be extended to working in partnership with parents and carers. This is unquestionably a challenging and complex area for development in educational establishments, as there are always so many reasons why this is limited so that the 'power' remains firmly in the hands of the educators. For children with special educational needs, in-depth and child-centred approaches to planning are required to take place with the parents or carers, and without a real even balance of power, these cannot really be truly effective. Targets need to be written together and provision and strategies agreed during structured conversations.

Following on from this, there is a section which focuses on working with other professionals, and how positive and collaborative ways of working can be formed. With a national focus on multi-professional working, the SENCO needs to be both knowledgeable and realistic about what others can do and when. You are challenged to consider how effectively you and your colleagues work, consult and engage with Governors, Trustees, volunteers and the wider community in the interest of practice and all learners, including those children and young people with complex special educational needs. Finally, this chapter also provides information about mediation and the SEND Tribunal.

### Chapter 7 A SENCO calendar

In this concluding chapter you will be shown how SENCOs can draw on the many elements discussed throughout this book to develop a three-year strategic plan for their educational institution or setting, owned not just by them, but by all involved in the specific community. Importantly the management of expectations and of their own well-being will be examined.

This chapter also emphasizes the importance of being realistic about what can be achieved by an individual SENCO and as an establishment. Time organization and time management are also discussed at this point, as is your acceptance that you need to see your role as leading strategic change.

# 1 The development of the SENCO role

**Introduction**

This first chapter is essential to read and engage with, whether you are new or a very experienced SENCO with actual personal experiences of living through the role's development. It is vital that you understand the current national expectations of the professional responsibilities of this role, because without this clarity, you will all too easily end up trying to be a multiple 'SENCO', fulfilling what various other people perceive to be the role rather than what it actually should be. There is nothing worse than trying to manage different expectations, and it usually leads to confusion, the duplication of tasks, dissatisfaction and, worse of all, a poor service to children, young people and their families.

What you will begin to recognize as you move through this chapter is that to be an effective SENCO at this point in time you have to be (and want to be) a leader within the education profession, able to develop and manage a whole school strategy and able to promote, enthuse and to drive forward change. However, to be a successful SENCO, you also need to have excellent interpersonal skills, to want to enable all children and young people, whatever their challenges, to learn and to want to have economic independence and the opportunity of a valuable role in society. You need to be persistent, organized, open to all, empathic, caring and to have a total belief in the empowerment of education to change lives.

A SENCO is now the only professional within an educational setting who has to be both a qualified teacher and to have a specific post-graduate qualification in order to hold and maintain a substantive role. The significance of this single factor suggests that the government is using the SENCO role and focused legislation, to bring about the changes they desire for as many children and young people as quickly as possible. In order to achieve this, SENCOs need to be able to see and own 'the big picture' and to know what will be achieved and improved as a consequence of this new approach. Without this vision and understanding of the need for collegiate ownership, anxiety among colleagues, children and young people, and parents will grow, and instead of finding ways to embed new systems and processes into and throughout an establishment, resistance will grow.

## 1.1 SEN legislation and policy

A decade ago, an independent House of Commons Select Committee Report (2006) provided the then Labour Government with a critical perspective on the national issues of special educational needs. The publication of this Report was significant, because it strongly suggested that SEN procedures and processes were 'outdated' and that the whole SEN system did not require further tweaks, but a complete overhaul. It highlighted that in England there was a problematic nature with SEN itself and a massive variation in SEN provision could be seen even between neighbouring schools, let alone those in different geographical areas. It went on to say that the position of special schools was uncertain and that all the SEN processes, including the 'statementing' process, were 'struggling to remain fit for purpose' (House of Commons Select Committee, 2006: 12). It is also significant that 20 years on from the landscape-changing Warnock Report (Warnock, 1978), Mary Warnock herself spoke in this report about regretting the introduction of the phrase 'special educational needs', saying:

> [O]ne of the major disasters of the original report was that we introduced the concept of special educational needs to try and show that disabled children were not a race apart and many of them should be educated in the mainstream . . . the unforeseen consequence is that SEN has come to be the name of a single category.
>
> (House of Commons, 2006: 16)

The first decade of the twenty-first century also saw alongside these issues a growing tension between the government's push for higher standards, focused on in the *National Strategies* materials, and the *Every Child Matters* (HM Treasury, 2003) agenda, focused on a broader, inclusive approach.

In response to the House of Commons Select Committee Report (2006), a number of new inquiries and regulations were quickly commissioned by the Labour Government. The Bercow Report (DCSF, 2008) and the Lamb Inquiry (DCSF, 2009a) re-emphasized previously identified issues such as:

> widely varying levels of parental confidence and . . . variation at local authority level in a wide range of different indicators: from overall levels of SEN and the SEN–non-SEN attainment gap, to levels of exclusions, the number of statements issued and the time in which they are issued.
>
> (DCSF, 2009a: 52)

For SENCOs, there was also the acknowledgement that the role needed to be held by qualified teachers and leaders able to engage in critical strategic work (HMSO, 2008; 2009). No longer could head teachers or governors decide to give this position to a teaching assistant or unqualified teacher. It had finally been recognized that a SENCO needs to have teaching experience, to have a teaching qualification and also the ability to achieve a postgraduate academic qualification. These regulations clearly indicated that the government wanted SENCOs to be able to command professional respect, and have leadership qualities and academic ability to help them make critical strategic decisions. Hence, between 2006 and 2010 the importance of parental confidence, the responsibilities of the role of the SENCO, and specific understanding and knowledge of the different areas of SENs began to be clearly voiced in review and research reports. They were to have a significant influence in changing the direction of travel for special educational needs legislation and requirements and indeed predicted some, at least, of the findings from the Ofsted Review, *Special Educational Needs and Disability Review: A Statement Is Not Enough* (Ofsted, 2010), commissioned by the outgoing Labour Government, this Review (Ofsted, 2010) reported back to a Coalition Government. The most shocking finding was the 'virtually unanimous feeling that the SEN system as it stands now is unfair: those who are able to make sense of it have quicker and greater access to resources and support' (Ofsted, 2010: 31). Once again, this Report expressed concerns about the variability in the identification of SEN between schools and local authorities. Like Warnock (House of Commons, 2006), it thought that the term 'special educational needs' was used in an indiscriminate manner, leading to the over-identification and incorrect identification of children and young people with a SEN. It suggested that, in some cases, additional, expensive provision was being used to make up for poor quality teaching and support. As in the Lamb Inquiry (DCSF, 2009a), this Review also highlighted the difficulties caused for parents, carers and children by the lack of collaboration and the confusing differences of language used by the statutory agencies. This Review also said that some schools, because of financial motivations such as formula funding and contextual value added scores, were also over-identifying pupils as having a SEN. Seeing such inequalities evolving in the system the Coalition Government published its Green Paper (DfE, 2011: 4) setting out a commitment to a 'radically different system to support better life outcomes for young people; give parents confidence by giving them more control; and transfer power to professionals on the front line and to local communities'. Not waiting for the final conclusions from *The Special Educational Needs and Disability Pathfinder Programme Evaluation Final Impact Research Report* (DfE, July 2015), the *Special Educational Needs and Disabilities Code of Practice: 0 to 25 Years* (DfE and DoH, 2014) was published in a rush by the then Secretary of State for Education, Michael Gove, in July 2014, a few weeks before its required implementation in local authorities and educational settings on 1st September 2014 when 'all the organisations listed in paragraph iv. **must** have regard to this Code of Practice' (DfE and DoH, 2015: 14). This statutory guidance underwent further amendments with additional specific information for youth custody and early years' provisions in January 2015 and then again in May 2015.

It is not understating the fact that the impact of the changes required within such a short period of time have been most intensely felt by SENCOs who have had to try to keep up with the national and local authority changes to processes and systems relating to SEN funding and support, let alone the new way of working and new level of responsibilities of their professional role. Add to this the new curriculum, assessment, examination and Ofsted requirements, it is explicitly clear why SENCOs have to be resilient, committed and exceptional education professionals. It is thus hoped that this manual will, first, help new SENCOs understand the changing legislation and practice environment and then develop a comprehensive strategic plan to help change practice and positively impact on outcomes for the children and young people they work with.

Table 1.1 provides a chronology of the significant legislation and practice relating to SEN up to and including the current *Special Educational Needs and Disability Code of Practice: 0 to 25 Years* (DfE and DoH, 2015).

**Table 1.1** Chronology of special educational needs inquiries, reviews and legislation

| *Year* | *Result* | |
|---|---|---|
| 2006 | House of Commons Select Committee (2006) | The SEN system is 'struggling to remain fit for purpose' (House of Commons, 2006: 12) |
| 2008 | *The Bercow Report* (DCSF, 2008) | The Bercow Report detailed findings from a review of services for children and young people (0–19) with speech, language and communication needs across England |
| 2008 | The Education (Special Educational Needs Coordinators) Regulations | This regulation required a SENCO to:<br>(a) be a qualified teacher;<br>(b) complete an induction period under regulations made under Section 19 of the Teaching and Higher Education Act 1998<br>(c) work as a teacher at the school |
| 2009 | *The Lamb Inquiry* (DCSF, 2009a) | Brian Lamb and the SEN Consortium were tasked to explore ways in which parental confidence in the SEN assessment process could be improved |
| 2009 | The Education (Special Educational Needs Co-ordinators (England) (Amended) Regulations (2009, No. 1387) | Since 2009, all new SENCOs have to complete the 'National Award for Special Educational Needs Co-ordination' within three years of taking up a post |
| 2010 | *The SALT Review* (DCSF, 2010a) | This Review investigated teacher supply issues relating to children with Severe Learning Difficulties and Profound and Multiple Learning Difficulties |
| 2010 | *Breaking the Link between Special Educational Needs and Low Attainment* (DCSF, 2010b) | This document discusses the need for identification of SEN to be individual, and followed by interventions that are tailored to meet the particular needs of a child |
| 2010 | *Improving Parental Confidence in the Special Educational Needs System: An Implementation Plan* (DCSF, 2010c) | This is the Implementation Plan which set out the then government's response to the 51 recommendations made by the Lamb Inquiry |
| 2010 | *The Importance of Teaching* (DfE, 2010) | This White Paper outlined a raft of the Coalition Government's measures for wide-reaching schools reform in England. It emphasized greater autonomy for schools and empowerment of teachers. It included plans to expand eligibility for Academy Schools and greater support for the establishment of new Free Schools. |
| 2010 | *Special Educational Needs and Disability Review: A Statement Is Not Enough* (Ofsted, 2010) | This is an Ofsted survey report which evaluated how well the legislative framework served children and young people with a SEN |

**Table 1.1** (continued)

| *Year* | *Result* | |
|---|---|---|
| 2011 | Green Paper, *Support and Aspiration: A New Approach to Special Educational Needs and Disability* (DfE, 2011) | This was a consultation paper which set out the Coalition Government's proposals to change the way help is given to children and young people with disabilities and/or special needs |
| 2014 | Children and Families Act (2014) | 'An Act to make provision about children, families, and people with special educational needs or disabilities; to make provision about the right to request flexible working; and for connected purposes.' |
| 2014/2015 | *Special Educational Needs and Disability Code of Practice: 0 to 25 Years* (DfE and DoH, 2014). This was subsequently updated in both January and May 2015 | This is the national guidance on the special educational needs and disability (SEND) system for children and young people aged 0 to 25, from 1 September 2014. It is 'Statutory guidance for organisations which work with and support children and young people who have special educational needs or disabilities.' |

## 1.2 Educational equality for children and young people with a special educational need and/or disability

It is beyond the space available to discuss inclusion, equality, equity and personalization in great detail in this book. However, it is vital that as a SENCO, you are actively involved in these current debates. How can we, for example, have really valuable debates about special educational needs if we are not clear about what 'Education for All' means or what educational equality should look like for all children and young people, including those with disabilities or a special educational need?

In the next few paragraphs, a specific perspective will be considered which hopefully will help you think about your own views and values and how these influence how you fulfil your role as a SENCO.

Despite the evolving and on-going debate about inclusive education throughout the last decade, the implementation of the former Special Educational Needs Code of Practice (DfES, 2001a) still meant that local authorities and schools, perhaps not surprisingly, placed great emphasis on the categorization of need of individual learners as a means of determining provision within an environment of ever-increasing financial constraints. This unfortunately led, it can be argued, to the 'labelling and devaluing [of] children and young people with disabilities and special educational needs' (Terzi, 2010: 39), despite the best intentions, and led to what some, including Norwich (2002: 495) term 'the dilemma of difference'. How many of you have heard colleagues or parents talk about the 'SEN children' or the 'autistic pupils' in less than positive ways, for example? And heard some asking questions such as why so many resources are directed towards children on the SEN register? Terzi (2010) explains that there is a tension between aiming to treat all learners the same, while supporting their individual needs by treating them differently. Clarifying further, she says that this debate reflects the opposing perspectives of the medical model the ('within-child' problems) and the social model, whereby the school system does not accommodate all children. This dilemma is illustrated in the Ofsted Review (2010), where it states that the SEN system in England was perpetuating unfairness and that the definitions of inclusion and special educational needs were continuing to be confused and to cause confusion. Try asking all your members of staff what they feel inclusive education is and I suspect that you will still, even in 2016, get a range of different answers.

In thinking about the 'dilemma of difference', Terzi (2010) engaged with the debate about what educational equality is for children and young people with a disability or special educational need in a western society, like England. Using the work of others, such as Sen (1980; 1992), Nussbaum (2000) and Rawls (2001), she suggests that the capability approach is a principled framework which 'substantially helps in conceptualizing educational equality by focusing on the fundamental educational capabilities that are essential prerequisites for functioning as an equal and effective participant in society' (Terzi, 2010: 164). She proposed a two-part framework, the first part of which states: 'equal opportunities for fundamental educational functionings [*should*] be provided at levels necessary to individuals for an effective participation in society' (Terzi, 2010: 163). This thinking clearly legitimizes additional resources being spent on children and young people with a disability or special educational need. The second part of this framework, however, states that when moving beyond the set level of the agreed fundamental functionings, resources should be spent in ways that 'allow the higher achievements of some to benefit those achieving at a lower level' (Terzi, 2010: 164). Terzi herself says that this framework does not provide a theory for what educational equality is, but she does wonder if it could help us to think about 'what constitutes educational equality' (2010: 164) for children and young people with a disability or a special educational need, and thus resolve the circular issues of the last 20 years or so.

**Practice questions**

- Do you agree that considering what educational equality constitutes for children and young people with a special educational need or disability is a valid argument?
- How does Terzi's capability approach fit within your views of educational equality and inclusive education?

## 1.3 Inclusive education and personalization

The definition of inclusion as stated earlier was and continues to be confusing. For some, inclusion relates to the physical placement of a child or young person, while, for others, it has a much broader role in enhancing social inclusion and social justice. The previous *Special Educational Needs Code of Practice* (DfES, 2001a) refers readers to the statutory framework for inclusion (Education Act, 1996, Section 316A) and directs schools to use the now defunct statutory guidance *Inclusive Schooling* (DfEs, 2001b) for advice and guidance when mentioning inclusion. This latter document set out seven principles of an inclusive education service and also informed schools how they should develop effective inclusion:

> Schools supported by local education authorities and others should actively seek to remove barriers to learning and participation that can hinder or exclude pupils with special educational needs . . . They also approach inclusion as part of their overall improvement strategy. Inclusion is far more than just about the location of a child's school placement. Inclusion is about engendering a sense of community and belonging and encouraging a sense of community and belonging.
>
> (DfES, 2001b: 2–3)

Further material such as the *Index for Inclusion* (Booth and Ainscow, 2002) and the National Curriculum 2000 emphasized the importance of providing effective opportunities for all through overcoming barriers to learning, supporting diversity and increasing access to learning.

The Coalition Government (2010–2015) stated that they would remove 'the bias towards inclusion' and although the current *Special Educational Needs and Disability Code of Practice: 0 to 25 Years* (DfE and DoH, 2015: 20) states that its principles support 'a focus on inclusive practice and removing barriers to learning', it only discusses this in relation to 'place' and 'admissions'.

So what is happening? Looking back, it can be said that despite all of the legislation and guidance materials, the speed of change towards inclusive education continued to be slow with teachers and educators still wanting 'others' to pay for and take responsibility for the learning of children and young people with special educational needs and/or disabilities. The children or young people with special educational needs were still too often considered the responsibility of the SENCO and others with specific SEN roles. The numbers of children and young people identified as requiring additional and different provision (especially School Action and School Action Plus) were increasing. It thus became very clear in the middle of the last decade that with greater challenging economic and social conditions, there was a need to develop an education system that could meet the needs of all pupils without a growing SEN separate system requiring additional funding and support. Undoubtedly there was also seen to be a need to raise standards of learning and achievement for all children to be able to sustain global markets in the future and that, once again, all teachers needed to be responsible for this as part of their role. Whether the driver was the desire for greater inclusion or national finances and economic success, it became important that the education system had to become more efficient, and focused 'on life outcomes, including employment and greater independence' (DfE and DoH, 2015: 11) for all.

Back in 1995, Len Barton (2010: 90) talked about the challenges which were 'integral to the process of change' and said that pursuing inclusive policies and practices would be 'serious, complex and contentious'. Barton continues, these challenges 'will include changes to the values informing the prioritization and distribution of resources, how society views difference, how schools are organized, how teachers view their work, the styles of their teaching and the nature of the curriculum'. Towards the end of the last decade, debate commenced which discussed equitable educational opportunities and what this should be for children and young people with special educational needs (see Section 1.2).

The current Conservative Government has continued with this process of change, noting the findings from reports such as Ofsted (2010) and the *Achievement for All National Evaluation* (Humphrey and Squires, 2011a) to refocus the responsibility for children and young people with a special educational need or disability away from SEN staff alone to that of all teachers and senior leaders using whole institutions' systems as a way of enforcing this way of working. The new Code of Practice (DfE and DoH, 2015: 25) therefore replaced the stage approach to the identification of SEN with a graduated approach, enforcing their belief that 'high quality teaching that is differentiated and personalized will meet the individual needs of the majority of children and young people' without additional and different provision. The focus also moved from concentrating on the provision provided to achieved outcomes, with greater emphasis on transitions to adult life, employment and independence. The personalization agenda which had been bubbling along for the past ten or so years at least also supported this change in approach regarding roles and responsibilities in the *Making Good Progress* (DfES, 2007a: 16) government (New Labour) consultation document saying that:

> The personalised classroom . . . is about having one strong inclusive teaching plan which allows as much room as possible for individual engagement, targeted support, a degree of choice and respect for the range of abilities and interests in the class. In the personalised classroom, it is recognised that all children have individual learning needs, not just those with Special Educational Needs. Hence with the changes in approach to the education system the role of the SENCO also had to dramatically change.

**Practice questions**

- Do you think that the change in approach towards special educational needs was necessary?
- Think carefully before moving onto the next section of this chapter about how:
  1. you see your role as a SENCO;
  2. the senior leaders or managers see the SENCO role;
  3. other nursery staff, teachers, or tutors see the SENCO role.

## 1.4 Roles and responsibilities of a SENCO

I first became a SENCO in 1995, a year after the original *Code of Practice on the Identification and Assessment of Special Educational Needs* (DfE, 1994) was published. Then, according to (DfE, 1994: 9–10). the SEN co-ordinator 'in all mainstream schools [should be] a designated teacher responsible for:

- the day-to-day operation of the school's SEN policy;
- liaising with and advising fellow teachers;
- co-ordinating provision for children with special educational needs;
- maintaining the school's SEN register and overseeing the records on all pupils with special educational needs;
- liaising with parents of children with special educational needs;
- contributing to the in-service training of staff;
- liaising with external agencies including the educational psychology service and other support agencies, medical and social services and voluntary bodies.

None of these responsibilities would be alien to today's SENCO, but the practice then was different. Interestingly at Stage 1 (of five Stages), the class or subject teacher was still responsible for identifying a child's special educational needs and for taking initial action.

However, in reality, this was often a quick conversation between the teacher and the SENCO in the corridor and a 'Would you please take a look at . . .?' As a SENCO, I would organize and teach individual and small groups of children outside of the classroom, as would any involved external agency. I would line-manage and organize a large group of teaching assistants who would provide individual or group support for children who were on the SEN register with the teacher (often again outside of the classroom). I would provide the resources and be responsible for the children's progress. If a child misbehaved, he or she would be sent to the SENCO to 'deal with' and I would be the one carrying out all of the assessments. Children being 'integrated' from special schools would do their 'own work' and the teacher would remain focused on working with the 'majority' who didn't need additional or different input and help. The other elements of the role were very similar; working with other agencies and with parents and carers, as well as undertaking in-service training for staff.

Very quickly, the role of SENCO became overwhelming with huge amounts of paperwork, teaching and meetings. It became impossible for one person to manage all of the tasks in some schools. The inclusion agenda was also gaining ground, along with a rights agenda for children and young people with special educational needs and/or disabilities and their parents/carers.

In January 2002, an updated *Special Educational Needs Code of Practice* (DfES, 2001a) was implemented. Early education settings were now also required to have a SENCO, according to the (DfES, 2001a: 34), who would be responsible for:

- liaison with other parents and other professionals in respect of children with special educational needs;
- advising and supporting other practitioners in the setting;
- ensuring that appropriate Individual Education Plans (IEP) are in place;
- ensuring that relevant background information about individual children with special educational needs is collected, recorded and updated.

When looking at the responsibilities of a SENCO in a primary school, the responsibilities remained the same with only one addition which reflected my personal experiences as a SENCO: 'managing learning support assistants' (LSA) (DfES, 2001a: 50).

However, there was now a whole chapter which looked at the 'identification, assessment and provision in the secondary sector' (DfES, 2001a: 59–73) specifically. Here instead of the responsibility to manage LSAs, the secondary school SENCO has the responsibility of 'managing the SEN team of teachers and learning support assistants' (DfES, 2001a : 65).

There was recognition that the SENCO role as it was evolving was time-consuming and required leadership skills. The chapters devoted to Early Education Settings, the Primary Sector and the Secondary Sector now all spoke about the time involved to fulfil this role: 'The role is time-consuming and therefore it is usually inappropriate for the SENCO to have other school-wide responsibilities' (DfES, 2001a: 51), and about the role's position within the establishment: 'Settings may find it effective for the SENCO to be a member of the senior management team' (DfES, 2001a: 35). DfES also stated: 'Many schools find it effective for the SENCO to be a member of the senior leadership team' (2001a: 51, 67).

This Code of Practice clearly indicated that it was the SENCO who was responsible for *co-ordinating* the best special educational needs provision for children and young people, not providing it. It also stated that children and young people with special educational needs should receive high quality teaching, ensuring 'that learning for all pupils is given equal priority, and that available resources are used to maximum effect' (DfES, 2001a: 65). Sections 5.2 and 6.2 reinforced the fact that 'provision for children with special educational needs is a matter for the school as a whole' and that 'All teachers are teachers of children with special educational needs' (DfES, 2001a : 44, 59), but it also said that 'in practice, the way in which this responsibility is exercised by individual staff is a matter for schools'. Thus, when teachers stated very loudly that they did not have the training or time to teach the children or young people with special educational needs, senior leaders decided to keep the status quo and required the SENCO to manage the education and progress of those with a SEN. Unfortunately, this also led in some cases to schools choosing to employ a teaching assistant (TA) to be the SENCO, to complete the paperwork and liaise with other professionals and parents.

With the need to raise standards for all and to use resources more effectively, it became obvious to governments that the SEN system (and hence the Code of Practice) were becoming unfit for purpose by the middle of the last decade. Lack of knowledge and skills about special educational needs in the general teaching workforce was recognized, as was the strength of a SENCO in leading and moving forward change. Thus, the new *Special Educational Needs and Disability Code of Practice: 0 to 25 Years* (DfE and DoH, 2015) has supported earlier legislation by stating explicitly that no longer should SENCOs be used as just a co-ordinator, but that they should determine the strategic development of an establishment's SEN policy and the provision: 'They will be most effective in that role [as SENCO] if they are part of the school leadership team' (DfE and DoH, 2015: 108).

The many other aspects of a SENCO's role as indicated in the previous Codes of Practice have been altered in the current Code of Practice to ensure that the

**Table 1.2** Roles and responsibilities of the SENCO

| *Type of provision/SENCO* | *Roles and responsibilities of the SENCO* |
|---|---|
| Early years provision (DfE and DoH, 2015: 5.54: 89) | • ensuring all practitioners in the setting understand their responsibilities to children with SEN and the setting's approach to identifying and meeting SEN<br>• advising and supporting colleagues<br>• ensuring parents are closely involved throughout and that their insights inform action taken by the setting<br>• liaising with professionals or agencies beyond the setting |
| Early years Area SENCOs (DfE and DoH, 2015: 5.56: 89–90) | • providing advice and practical support to early years providers about approaches to identification, assessment and intervention within the SEND Code of Practice<br>• providing day-to-day support for setting-based SENCOs in ensuring arrangements are in place to support children with SEN<br>• strengthening the links between the settings, parents, schools, social care and health services<br>• developing and disseminating good practice<br>• supporting the development and delivery of training both for individual settings and on a wider basis<br>• developing links with existing SENCO networks to support smooth transitions to school nursery and receptions classes<br>• informing parents of and working with local impartial Information, Advice and Support Services, to promote effective work with parents of children in the early years |
| Mainstream schools/ academy schools/ free schools SENCO (DfE and DoH, 2015: 6.90: 108–9) | • overseeing the day-to-day operation of the school's SEN policy<br>• co-ordinating provision for children with SEN<br>• liaising with the relevant Designated Teacher where a looked after pupil has SEN<br>• advising on the graduated approach to providing SEN support<br>• advising on the deployment of the school's delegated budget and other resources to meet pupils' needs effectively<br>• liaising with parents of pupils with SEN<br>• liaising with early years providers, other schools, educational psychologists, health and social care professionals, and independent or voluntary bodies<br>• being a key point of contact with external agencies, especially the local authority and its support services<br>• liaising with potential next providers of education to ensure a pupil and their parents are informed about options and a smooth transition is planned<br>• working with the head teacher and school governors to ensure that the school meets its responsibilities under the Equality Act (2010) with regard to reasonable adjustments and access arrangements<br>• ensuring that the school keeps the records of all pupils with SEN up to date |
| Further education colleges, sixth form colleges and 16–19 academies (named | • to have oversight of SEN provision to ensure co-ordination of support<br>• to contribute to the strategic and operational management of the college |

(*Continued*)

**Table 1.2** (continued)

| *Type of provision/SENCO* | *Roles and responsibilities of the SENCO* |
|---|---|
| person for SEN similar to SENCO in schools) (DfE and DoH, 2015: 7.22: 116–17) | • curriculum and support staff in a college should know who to go to if they need help in identifying a student's SEN, are concerned about their progress or need further advice |
| Children (under 16) and Young People (over 16) in Youth Custody Accommodation (SENCO) (DfE and DoH, 2015: 10.73: 225; 10.77: 226) | • to be part of key personnel delivering the detained person's sentence plan<br>• providers should meet the educational needs of all detained persons, including those with SEN, whether they have an EHC plan or not<br>• ensure SEN provision, identification and support of SEN follows the model (for schools and colleges)<br>• have staff who are suitably qualified to support this (such as SENCOs) and make referrals to other specialist support where this is appropriate<br>• liaise and co-operate with the local authority where a detained person has an EHC plan |
| *Additional note*<br>Designated Teacher for looked after children (DfE and DoH, 2015: 10.3: 209) | • All maintained and academies and free schools must appoint a Designated Teacher for looked after children. Where that role is carried out by a person other than the SEN Co-ordinator (SENCO), Designated Teachers should work closely with the SENCO to ensure that the implications of a child being both looked after and having SEN are fully understood by relevant school staff |

SENCO is to be considered a point of contact or an advisor, rather than the professional who has the responsibility to carry out the actions alone. SENCOs must also be a qualified teacher in maintained nurseries and schools, and in further education,

> [Colleges] should ensure that there is a named person in the college with oversight of SEN provision to ensure co-ordination of support, similar to the role of the SEN Co-ordinator (SENCO) in schools. This person should contribute to the strategic and operational management of the college.
>
> (DfE and DoH, 2015: 116–17)

Importantly, and emphasizing the strategic leadership aspect of the role, all new SENCOs 'must achieve a National Award in Special Educational Needs Co-ordination within three years of appointment' (DfES, 2001a: 108). Table 1.2 provides an overview of the roles and responsibilities of SENCOs in different types of education establishment.

SENCOs are now the only member of a maintained nursery or school setting who have to be a qualified teacher and have to have a postgraduate qualification. What an accolade and what a responsibility. SENCOs are considered by the government to be an essential strategic and operational leader and manager of an educational establishment, who are being given the responsibility of ensuring that nurseries, schools and colleges are actively engaged in the diversity, equality and inclusion agendas as they develop and enhance practices and policies.

## What does this mean for the SENCO?

- *Essentially, it means that as a SENCO you must understand the Special Educational Needs and Disability Code of Practice: 0 to 25 Years (DfE and DoH, 2015) thoroughly and how the local authority or other local or national group (e.g. multi-academy trusts) interpret the Code for local needs.*
- *As a SENCO, you need to understand that your role is a strategic whole school development one, with aspects of operational responsibility as well.*
- *SENCOs need to work as part of or through the Senior Leadership Team (SLT) of an educational establishment to ensure that all processes, policies, resourcing and systems support the tracking and recording of all children and young people, including those with special educational needs and/or disability.*
- *SENCOs are not the ones who have the lone responsibility of working directly with all the children and young people on the SEN register; that is the responsibility of all teachers.*
- *SENCOs are not the ones with lone responsibility for the progress of children and young people with a special educational need and/or a disability; that is the responsibility of all teachers.*
- *All members of the educational establishment need to understand that the SENCO will not have the answers to all the concerns or needs of all children, but that they will be the ones to ensure that the resources required (including training for staff) are available for the children and young people.*

## Direct links to the SEND Code of Practice

- 5.52 A maintained nursery school must ensure that there is a qualified teacher designated as the SENCO in order to ensure the detailed implementation of support for children with SEN.
- 5.53 The EYFS framework requires other early years providers to have arrangements in place for meeting children's SEN. Those in group provision are expected to identify a SENCO. Childminders are encouraged to identify a person to act as SENCO.
- 5.55 The Area SENCO helps make the links between education, health and social care to facilitate appropriate early provision for children with SEN and their transition to compulsory schooling.
- 6.85 The SENCO must be a qualified teacher working at the school. A newly appointed SENCO must be a qualified teacher and, where they have not previously been a SENCO at that or any other relevant school for a total period of more than twelve months, they must achieve a National Award in Special Educational Needs Co-ordination within three years of appointment.
- 7.22 Colleges . . . should ensure that there is a named person in the college with oversight of SEN provision to ensure co-ordination of support, similar to the role of the SEN Co-ordinator (SENCO) in schools.

# 2 Leading, developing and supporting colleagues

For many years the SENCO has been the colleague to whom teachers go if they have concerns about a child or young person with special educational needs. Too often the SENCO, who was often in a middle management-type role, would say 'Leave it with me' or 'Yes, I will do this/complete the form', and so on. I will admit to personally taking on many such requests without question. SENCOs would be the ones to manage support staff, all SEN-related meetings and additional support in the classroom – perhaps even the curriculum for a particular child or young person. Although this level of individual responsibility is not the current expectation, a SENCO or named person with SEN oversight clearly does still have operational tasks to fulfil (Table 2.1).

However, at all stages of a child's and young person's educational experience a person with SEN responsibility or oversight is now required by legislation and guidance to take on a strategic and thus leadership role in all maintained nurseries, maintained schools, free schools and academies, and colleges. This is particularly transparent as the Code of Practice (DfE and DoH, 2015: 6.91: 109) says:

> The school should ensure that the SENCO has sufficient time and resources to carry out these functions. This should include providing the SENCO with sufficient administrative support and time away from teaching to enable them to fulfil their responsibilities in a similar way to other important strategic roles within a school.

So how do current SENCOs get the balance right between managing and leading? How do you ensure that you are still not stopped in the corridors and asked to solve a problem immediately or 'sent' all of the children or young people who need immediate support outside of a classroom? Over the past few years, strategies have been used to help SENCOs make these changes and these will be shared in this chapter. What is important to remember, though, is that you cannot do it all. You also need to be clear about in which elements of your work you are the manager and in which you are a leader. I suggest that understanding the differences in these roles will really help you to organize your workload and also help you delegate to others daily aspects of the role. You might need to have help to develop your communication skills, to know more about personnel regulations or even to gain confidence in your own abilities! Whatever it is, make sure you are aware of your areas for development and ask for support in achieving your goals. Also recognize that it is still important to have time outside of your professional role if you are not going to experience what we term 'burn-out'. Remember, if this happens, you will not be useful to any child or young person.

**Table 2.1** Type of SENCO and their duties

| *Type of SENCO* | *Duties* |
|---|---|
| Area SENCO in early years' provision: | Providing day-to-day support for setting-based SENCOs in ensuring arrangements are in place to support children with SEN (DfE and DoH, 2015: 5.56: 89) |
| School SENCO | Co-ordinating provision for children with SEN (DfE and DoH, 2015: 6.90: 108) |
| Named person with SEN oversight in colleges | They should ensure that there is a named person in the college with oversight of SEN provision to ensure co-ordination of support, similar to the role of the SEN Co-ordinator (SENCO) in schools. This person should contribute to the strategic and operational management of the college (DfE and DoH, 2015: 7.22: 116–17). |

## 2.1 Leadership

So what are the differences between being a leader and a manager and how can SENCOs effectively be a leader, a manager and also often an administrator, all at the same time? Interestingly, the literature over quite a period of time has also shown that this difficulty is not specific only to SENCOs in educational establishments:

> Schools leaders [experience] tensions between competing elements of leadership, management and administration. Irrespective of how these terms are defined, school leaders experience difficulty in deciding the balance between higher order tasks designed to improve staff, student and school performance (leadership), routine maintenance of present operations (management) and lower order duties (administration).
>
> (Dimmock, 1999: 442)

Cuban (1988: xx) provides what I feel is a very clear definition of leadership when he writes: 'Leaders are people who shape the goals, motivations, and actions of others. Frequently they initiate change to reach existing and new goals . . . Leadership . . . takes . . . much ingenuity, energy and skill.' However, as with many other terms, there is not only not a single or correct definition of leadership, but there are many different forms of leadership as well (Bush, 2003). Indeed, within our field of practice, the notions of shared leadership or moral leadership are frequently prominent, with the term 'inclusive leadership' (Ekins, 2012: 168) appearing in recent years. Ekins (2012: 168) describes key elements of this style of leadership as including:

- a shared vision
- commitment

- collaboration
- communication.

The 'Achievement for All' framework (www.afaeducation.org.charity) (accessed 1 August 2016) also embeds this shared style of leadership within its materials, stating: 'School leaders at various levels of leadership and not just headship – will provide the vision, strategic planning, motivation, support, resources, structures and environment for learning that enable staff in schools and other children's services . . .' (National College, 2010: 3).

**Practice questions**

- So how would you describe your education establishment's style of leadership?
- How supportive of the work of the SENCO is it?
- Do the definitions above help you understand why you are either included or not included in the leadership group of your establishment?
- Do you or can you influence the future direction of the leadership group within your own place of work?

So what part of the SENCO role is a managerial one? One definition of a manager is a person whose 'overall function is toward maintenance rather than change' (Cuban, 1988: xx). A manager is someone who works within current structures and practices in an organization. A manager aims to be effective and efficient, but maintains rather than changes. Thus being a manager is clearly ensuring that all of the practical aspects of providing a child or young person with special educational needs, with personalized and aspirational education, is paramount. Note, though, it is ensuring it is achieved, not that the SENCO does it all.

From these definitions you can see why a SENCO needs to be described both as a strategic leader and a manager. As a SENCO, you are the crucial professional in developing the inclusion agenda further, at a good pace within your establishment, but you also have to ensure that all of the processes and procedures required by government are in place and are running smoothly to provide children and young people with SEN with the best possible holistic education. The combination of these roles is vital, and I strongly advocate they must not be 'watered down' by you having to undertake very routine, administrative jobs. As the SENCO, you can manage another colleague to do these administrative tasks, releasing you to focus on essential professional roles. It must not be forgotten that both leading and managing, while distinct, are very important for a SENCO to achieve successfully (Bolman and Deal, 1997: xiii–xiv):

> Organisations which are over-managed but under-led eventually lose any sense of spirit or purpose. Poorly managed organisations with strong charismatic leaders may soar temporarily only to crash shortly thereafter. The challenge of

modern organisations requires the objective perspective of the manager as well as the flashes of vision and commitment wise leadership provides.

If you think about educational establishments currently, I am sure you can immediately place your own and others in one or another of these situations. As a SENCO, you clearly want to be part of an educational establishment where your and others' 'combined' roles enable it to function as described in the final sentence of the quotation above.

**Practice suggestions**

To help you think about this in a more practical manner, go through the following documents, writing down all of the tasks you are expected to complete as part of the SENCO role:

- diary or calendar;
- SEND Code of Practice (DfE and DoH, 2015);
- your own job description with role and responsibility specifications;
- minutes of meetings.

Then alongside all of these tasks, write down whether they are part of your leadership, managerial or administrative role.

Then ask the questions:

- Looking at your nursery (provision), school or college development plan, is this division of your roles appropriate?
- If yes, how long for?
- If no, what needs to change and how can you achieve this?
- Who and what need to change?

I cannot provide a clear percentage figure of what each section of your workload will look like, because this will vary from establishment to establishment, depending on their stage of development. This could also vary over a three- or five-year period and I strongly recommend that you carry out this strategic work together with other senior leadership colleagues, especially if, for example, a large percentage of your time is spent carrying out administrative tasks. It is also fine to have an imbalance between managerial and leadership tasks, because, again, this will fluctuate, depending on the whole school development and many other factors, such as changes to staffing, legislation and local requirements, as well as resourcing and the community. This is why flexibility, communication and collaboration within a leadership team are so influential within any educational establishment.

Finally, don't forget about your own development within this complex situation. The roles and responsibilities of a SENCO are diverse and one person cannot be expected to be able to have all of the skills and knowledge immediately. Just look at the key responsibilities of the SENCO as detailed for schools in the SEND

Code of Practice (DfE and DoH, 2015: 6.90: 108–9). You are expected to do the following:

- know about budgets;
- understand and know the value (financial and professional) of the vast range of resources and strategies available for use with children and young people with special educational needs;
- have a wide range of interpersonal skills, including tone of voice, understanding about personal space, body language and sensitivity towards others' emotional engagement;
- communicate effectively with a wide range of stakeholders. This can be especially complex when working with parents/carers and includes how you communicate, e.g. email, text or other forms of written messages. How do you, for example, tell parents less positive news?
- know how to be assertive and how assertive to be;
- manage conflict and emotional distress;
- be a good report writer;
- be able to undertake and write up research studies;
- be a great organizer of provision, people and paperwork.

How many of us are very competent at all these things in an ever-evolving world where communication is instant? Therefore, be realistic, and while carrying out the practice suggestions above, include a column where you note down professional development you require in the short, medium and long term. Table 2.2 provides a possible format to undertake this assessment of your role, incorporating additional information which can be added to the whole school development plan and continuing professional development requirements. Do not forget to consider the frequency of the tasks, as this can quickly alter the implementation of a plan and its subsequent success.

**Table 2.2** Assessment of the SENCO roles and responsibilities

| *Task* | *Frequency of task* | *Leader (L), manager(M) or administrator (A)* | *Actions required* | *Continuing professional development (CPD)* |
|---|---|---|---|---|
| Reviewing the SEND policy | Annual | L | Ensure this is placed in planning to enable all stakeholders to be involved in a timely manner | None |
| To collect, comment and feed back to support staff about their record sheets | Monthly | M/A | For teachers, then year/subject heads to review these on a monthly basis. SENCO then to only view on a termly basis | Discussion with teachers and year heads about expectations |

## 2.2 Quality teaching and learning for all pupils

As the government reminded us in July 2014 and then again when the SEND Code of Practice was amended (DfE and DoH, 2015: 6.36, 6.37: 99), all teachers 'are responsible and accountable for the progress and development of the pupils in their class(es) including where pupils access support from teaching assistants or specialist staff' and 'high quality teaching, differentiated for individual pupils, is the first step in responding to pupils who have or may have SEN.' This, I strongly suggest, should be the same in all educational establishments and for all children and young people, whatever their age.

So what does a high quality class or room look like when considering children and young people with special educational needs? There are certain practices and resources all SENCOs will want to see in all rooms, whether early years, school age or college.

First, the environment itself is crucial and, as leaders, SENCOs are responsible for helping and ensuring resources are available to provide a comfortable, secure and effective learning space for all learners. A very useful method of looking at this at the whole school level is to undertake an environmental learning walk with a group of stakeholders each year. This group could include:

- a teacher from each part of the establishment;
- the SEN governor;
- parents of children or young people with and without SEN and/or a disability;
- pupils, perhaps from the School Council (including those with a SEN and/or disability);
- the head teacher.

This will provide a very holistic and general overview of the environment for all learners. Noisy floors, lack of window coverings or fresh air and lighting can be discussed during such walks, as well as space and specialist equipment for children or young people, staff, parents or visitors with a physical disability. Hopefully such a learning and environmental walk will also identify aspects of whole school provision which need to change, such as inappropriate-sized cutlery (e.g. nursery or reception-aged children being expected to use adult cutlery) and desks and chairs. This regular update can then be fed back into the business and access plans. Of course, such work will also help to inform stakeholders about the role the environment plays in supporting and enabling learning.

However, as SENCO, you also need to discuss this whenever necessary with each nursery nurse/teacher/tutor. Thus, it is vital you have a clear understanding (perhaps established following an audit of skills) about how much all teachers know about the impact of their use of the room and equipment for children or young people with special educational needs (and disabilities). As SENCO, part of your initial and on-going discussions with teachers (and all support staff), including during progress review meetings, should look at the environment from the perspective of all the people in the room, because this will immediately resolve a number of issues which will also be impacting on the learning of the children or young people with special educational needs. This will ensure each colleague has a sound understanding of what a good learning environment should look like. An example of this could be the seating arrangements. Who can see the computer or white screen straight on and from which positions? Have you considered the needs of those with visual or hearing difficulties or the children who are left-handed? Have you thought about the children or young people who need to have physical boundaries or need to feel well organized?

There are a number of excellent assessments which you can purchase or access to help you carry out an environmental survey of areas for particular SEN needs. These include the Autism Education Trust Sensory Assessment Checklist: http://www.aettraininghubs.org.uk/wp-content/uploads/2012/05/37.2-Sensory-assessment-checklist.pdf (accessed 28 February 2016) and the Leicestershire County Council Promoting Positive Environment Checklist which focuses especially on the environment and behaviour: http://www.leics.gov.uk/learning_environment_checklist_-_2007_version.pdf (accessed 28 February 2016).

What other generic quality teaching tools would you expect to see in each room in your establishment? This list, I suspect, would include:

- visual timetables;
- topic vocabulary on the walls (with symbols);
- all cupboards, drawers and parts of the room/environment labelled with words and symbols (pictures) that are age-appropriate;
- a variety of equipment readily available for use by all, e.g. sloping boards, wobble cushions, comfy cushions, foot rests and weighted shoulder or lap blankets, electronic spelling or writing aids and specialist writing equipment.

**Practice questions**

- Is there a resource which you feel all staff would be able to use very easily which you would want to purchase?
- What change would you like to introduce or reinforce first?
- Not every change needs expensive resources. Try to think of one thing you can improve in the learning environment which would cost nothing or very little.

**Practice suggestions**

- Make a list of resources you have in each room/classroom which aid all learners, including those with SEN. Only include those that are used regularly by the teacher or tutor.

Then when the general classroom potential issues have been discussed, you can begin to investigate the needs of individual children or young people. Try using the four areas of need as described in the *SEND Code of Practice: 0 to 25 Years*

(DfE and DoH, 2015: 6.28–6.35: 97–8) to help you and the teacher critically consider any possible required changes.

**Practice suggestions**

Provide each teacher with a table using the four areas of need as a separate headings:

1 Communication and interaction
2 Cognition and learning
3 Social, emotional and mental health difficulties
4 Sensory and/or physical needs

Then through discussion you can identify the children or young people who continue to need additional support over and above the universal inclusive resources and strategies. By honing in on what continues to be a barrier, you can then determine whether an additional assessment in one particular area of development is required, a small additional change to the learning environment is still needed, or whether there is a longer-term need. This will probably provide you with a great deal of qualitative evidence and additional quantitative data on which to base further explorations.

It is also important to be able to evidence high quality learning for children and young people with special educational needs. As a SENCO, you must work with the other leaders in the establishment to ensure that the assessments, data and processes used to measure the progress of all do exactly that. Once more, the *SEND Code of Practice: 0 to 25 Years* (DfE and DoH, 2015: 6.38: 99) provides a brief explanation:

> In deciding whether to make special educational provision, the teacher and SENCO should consider all of the information gathered from within the school about the pupil's progress, alongside national data and expectations of progress. This should include high quality and accurate formative assessment, using effective tools and early assessment materials.

This leads us on to discuss the employment and development of staff which is, I consider, a vital piece of this ever-changing and evolving puzzle. The Code of Practice clearly states that teachers have the responsibility and accountability for both the progress and development of the children or young people in their groups, classes or sessions, including the times when they are supported by teaching assistants or specialist SEN professionals. As SENCO, you thus need to proactively provide teachers, nursery staff or tutors with access to the knowledge and skills all need in order to fulfil this requirement. According to the *SEND Code of Practice: 0 to 25 Years* (DfE and DoH, 2015: 6.37: 99): 'High quality teaching, differentiated for individual pupils, is the first step to responding to' the needs of pupils with (or without) SEN. If further support is needed after this, the Code of Practice says that the four-part cycle, labelled the Graduated Approach, should be put in place. I would argue, however, that in order to achieve this graduated approach effectively, and to provide a clear analysis of a child's or young person's needs, the professionals do need a level of knowledge about atypical learning development to effectively identify and assess specific special educational needs. Without this, an important comment made by a parent or a specialist to the group, class or subject teacher may be completely ignored, and as SENCO you cannot be in every meeting or every class all of the time. Thus, the knowledge and expertise within your establishment need to be first known and then constantly developed and nurtured.

## 2.3 The employment and development of staff

### The development of staff

Unfortunately, this aspect of the SENCO or any other senior leadership role is frequently ad hoc or extremely low on the list of priorities. However, when working in the SEN field of practice, confidence and direct on-going training are key to ensuring the best is achieved for each child or young person. It is for this reason that I am starting this section of the chapter with the development of current staff rather than the employment of new staff. So how do you, first, get and then keep SEN and inclusion on the whole school development agenda?

**Practice questions**

- Do you have a current list of qualifications, interests and experiences of all staff in your establishment?
- Do you know the career aspirations of your staff?
- Who has access to this information and who is coordinating the training or opportunities which might enable the achievement of these?
- Where are the SEN knowledge and experience gaps?
- Is this an issue which impacts *significantly*, *slightly* or *not at all* on your current practice and cohort?
- Which professionals have SEND expertise?
- Are these the right professionals to have these skills and the knowledge when you look at the requirements within the SEND Code of Practice?
- How often does your senior leadership or management group discuss whole school rather than curriculum-focused skill sets?
- How frequently and where is continuing professional development (CPD) for SEND specifically mentioned in your establishment's development or self-evaluation plans?

The list of questions above will help you assess where you need to start your conversations with the other senior staff.

As with all other aspects of a SENCO role, a 360° view and plan are required to really enable you to embed an effective and sustainable process.

First, you need to compare your practice question answers to the needs of your children or young people on the SEN register, your medical conditions register, and, if you have one, your register of those you consider to be vulnerable. How equal are they? Where are there gaping holes or a high level of knowledge and skills? What does this tell you about your staff skill set and how this might impact on their understanding and knowledge of interventions, or methods of analysis? Does this align with strategies in use in classrooms and for targeted and specialist (individualized) programmes for children and young people with special educational needs?

Second, you need to see which group of professionals has the best SEN knowledge, skills and experience. Are they the support staff, the teachers or tutors, the SENCO or senior management? Is this a profile for your establishment which shows the right people have the right knowledge and skills? Remember who the SEND Code of Practice (DfE and DoH, 2015: 6.36: 99) says has the 'responsibility and accountability' for the progress and development of all children and young people at all times. Has there been a great reliance or even over-reliance on external expertise because of internal difficulties or is it not on the whole school agenda at all?

Third, you need to map the SEND training undertaken within the past five years. Has this been all in-house, on-line or external; has it been all staff or only specific individuals; and how great has the turnover of staff been. This also all needs to be costed so that you can begin to create a picture of whether this has been cost-effective, as well as positive for staff. Most importantly, has it impacted on the progress of the children or young people with special educational needs?

From this three-step action enquiry you can create an evaluation of current practice together with an action plan to present to the senior or management teams and governors or trustees. You will be able to demonstrate:

- the possible impact of correct/incorrect skill sets of staff on the progress of children or young people with special educational needs. This can be levelled, providing a picture of the different professionals working in your establishment;
- the financial cost of this (positive or negative) over a period of time can be mapped alongside the point above;
- a proposed training programme over the next three years (with the understanding that staff movement and change of child or young person intake will require annual adjustment) with costings and how this will impact on the progress of the children and young people with SEND. This should include a blend of routes and academic levels from whole school INSET presented by the SENCO to individual research qualifications (e.g. Ed.D or PhD).

In your report I suggest that you also:

- include direct links to the SEND Code of Practice, identifying the governing body's (senior leadership) responsibilities as well;
- use this opportunity to readjust how much of the budget the establishment spends on different groups of professionals involved in the success and

progress of children and young people with SEN. For example, with more of the budget spent on specific assessments and their implementation in school by school staff, would this save money and time by lessening the reliance on external specialists within a two- or three-year period?
- show how skills and knowledge gained to support and enable children and young people with a learning or development need, e.g. understanding the importance of attachment or emotional well-being on cognitive or motor development, will also improve educators' practice for all. The use of 'structured conversations' or the completion of a piece of action research are other such examples.
- indicate where and how specialist knowledge needs to be gathered and used, e.g. at point of employment and during performance management.

### Employment of staff

The most important thing to remember here is that it is better not to appoint at all than to appoint a person with the wrong skill set or a vision that does not match that of your establishment. To help achieve the successful appointment of a member of the support, teaching/tutor or senior management team, preparation and planning are key. Using all of the information gathered from your staffing evaluation and action plan, write a job description and person specification that will clearly indicate to any perspective applicant which skills and experience you are looking for. Do this in liaison with your business/human resources colleagues to ensure that aspects of the job description do not later cause you unnecessary difficulties. This could be especially important when you employ support staff. The following factors might help you when completing this task. Be clear about factors such as:

- whether they might be required to move around the school as determined by the head teacher/leader/senior manager;
- the fact that tasks might change depending on the needs of the children or young people, e.g. individual/small group work etc.;
- timing. This is frequently an issue for SENCOs who inherit a team of support staff who have always started at 9.30 a.m. and finish at 2 p.m. Be clear that although their hours might remain static, equally timings might change (in negotiation of course).
- meetings attendance and participation (e.g. progress review, planning meetings), INSET attendance and the completion and quality of paperwork required (literacy and numeracy skills);
- the duration and flexibility of the contract. This is essential as funding might have to stop or change almost immediately (e.g. if a child leaves your establishment) due to the current funding arrangements.
- if there is a necessity to undertake training which might require them to study outside of their contractual hours (and whether there is any compensation for this).

Undoubtedly there may be other factors which are specific to your own situation, but being very clear and specific from the outset will help you find the colleague you are looking for through clear criteria (essential and desirable) and enable you to also provide detailed feedback to unsuccessful applicants.

I also suggest that part of an interview session should involve seeing the applicants working with or being interviewed by the children or young people. Even if they have not worked in an educational establishment before, you need to see how they relate to the children and how they work with other adults. An educational environment is not for everyone, especially if it is a specialist environment. I know that when I was working in a special school, we used to say that new staff would either stay a morning, a week or a long time.

As SENCO, you might also be required to commission specific pieces of work necessitating the temporary or flexible employment of professionals from other disciplines. Again, think carefully about the actual outcomes you want to achieve before you start to advertise for a post. Also think about the level of expertise and experience required. For example, do not advertise for or appoint a professional who is newly qualified if you need them to work independently and with children or young people with complex difficulties. Also consider what type of environment this professional would normally be expected to work in within their discipline's framework. This is essential when thinking of employing colleagues who would perhaps be clinic-based and working either on a 1:1 specialist basis with a 'patient' or with very small groups. Asking them to work at the universal level in whole classes may thus be extremely challenging and very uncomfortable. If such situations are not thoroughly explored prior to appointment, unnecessary resignations and expense might be the outcome.

There is also the importance of recognizing that professionals from other disciplines may be required to attend specific annual professional training to enable them to remain registered within their profession. Others may need to have regular supervision sessions, all of which your establishment might end up funding, either in actual costs or in time. Additionally, if a therapist works as an independent consultant, you need to ensure that they are personally accessing continuing professional development with colleagues before you employ them so that you can be confident that their knowledge and skills are current and informed by research and their professional standards. As a SENCO, you need to take time to do this work thoroughly, especially if you are thinking of employing staff outside of the local NHS, social care or education services.

The induction process is also vital and it should include time for you and the SENCO to go through the school information report, the Local Offer and any resources, interventions and strategies all staff are expected to use. Other paperwork and meeting requirements should also be carefully explained so that expectations are clear from the beginning. This should hopefully enable the new member of staff to settle in quickly and also provide high quality input for all children and young people immediately.

## 2.4 Performance management

For many SENCOs, undertaking performance management for teaching colleagues and other staff such as teaching assistants and learning mentors requires new skills. As a SENCO in a large establishment, there might be a large number of support staff as well as technicians and teachers. As a senior leader, you should not be expected to undertake everyone's performance management and thus a clear line of responsibility for this should be introduced and mapped on your annual diary to ensure that this is completed on time and in a respectful and thorough manner. Many teachers now carry out performance management for their support staff, and year/team leads complete their teacher performance management. SENCOs should also be fully involved in this process with questions about SEN and inclusion included in all the documentation for all levels of staff monitoring. As SENCO, it is often very positive to complete the performance management process with group leaders and subject or year heads. In this way you can quickly ascertain the effectiveness of the establishment's SEN policy, its processes and practices.

When done well, both the member of staff and manager recognize how motivating and helpful such a process can be. They will be able to see how it connects to promotion (internal or external), training opportunities or even a planned, supportive exit! Unfortunately, again, in a busy establishment, this is often only paid lip service to. Links to teaching observations and peer reviews are also beneficial, again requiring the calendar to be planned a year in advance, but powerful in the quality of information gathered and shared. When filling in the calendar for the year, think of a possible timeframe between, for example, peer reviews and the annual performance management and add at least another couple of weeks. Also think about when during the year you should carry out performance management. Is it always best to time this for the end of the academic year? Do you have a half-yearly or new academic year catch-up to revisit targets and goals and to reinvigorate the team?

I suspect that most SENCOs like to encourage, motivate and be a manager who provides carrots or cake for encouragement, but, as leaders, SENCOs now have to be prepared and able to carry out the least positive aspects of the role. This might involve SENCOs giving staff formal warnings, carrying out safeguarding inquiries or even removing them from their positions. This is where initial contracts, performance management processes and close liaison with business colleagues can really help you know that you are fulfilling your responsibilities in the best possible way. It is probably one of the most unpleasant elements of the SENCO's senior leadership role, but I always find that remembering the following helps me to put everything in context, despite all the other practical aspects your decision might impact on for an individual and his or her family: 'A child only has one chance of an education and every day is part of that opportunity.' Also remember any such decision will not be your decision alone. It will be a collaborative decision made with a wealth of information and a genuine wish to get the best outcome for all.

## 2.5 Inspection

Always be ready for an inspection. The first point of call for any inspector will be the nursery, school or college website (if appropriate), so ensure that the SEN Information Report (or SEN Information) (and SEN Policy if it is separate) are up to date, easily accessible for all readers and include all the details as expressed in Section 6.79 of the SEND Code of Practice (DfE and DoH, 2015: 106). Also ensure that in this you mention the strengths of your establishment as stated in the last Ofsted report or other inspection. Provide the link to the local authority Local Offer. Do not forget about the Dash Board information either when relevant.

This is the first 'view' of the establishment, but how else can you ensure that you are ready at all times? The management part of the SENCO role is key here through a strong SEN administration system which routinely enables the collection of information and data by all in an agreed manner. Hopefully such a system, either paper-based or electronic, will include an invaluable SEN administrator or SEN assistant as well who can have daily and weekly responsibilities to update notices, provide diary information and make timely appointments. This colleague will also need to be part of the planning and organization process for meetings and to ensure all SEN requirements are fulfilled, as stated on the SENCO and school calendar as discussed earlier and in Chapter 6. This assistant will be able to ensure a portfolio is also in place with all of the most recent information and data included, detailing the progress of the children or young people with SEN. Indeed, some of you will have completed a portfolio of practice as part of your National Award for SEN Co-ordination. If kept current, this could provide you with the 'first' contact information for any inspector, detailing clearly how you fulfil all the roles and responsibilities of a SENCO as detailed in the Code of Practice.

With an assistant, this is easy to establish within an academic year and will give you the time to provide the strategic overview required to evidence the effectiveness of your leadership in establishing outstanding provision for children and young people with special educational needs.

Without an assistant, the ability to be ready for inspection needs a pragmatic approach which considers the time you have available on a weekly basis and the tasks you as SENCO are required to complete as directed by the Governing/Trust Body and your head teacher/manager. This pragmatic approach can be evidenced through your action plan in which you can show you know what needs to be done, but that it has to fit in with the pattern of the establishment and the available time. This will provide any inspector with confidence that you know what and how to implement change. This would relate to changes in practice such as the introduction of provision mapping and daily support staff learning journals or target sheets through to staff training and the implementation of new interventions or assessments.

Whatever you change or create, always think about how you can evidence the reasons for these changes in relation to the SEND Code of Practice (DfE and DoH, 2015) and how they comply with inspection requirements (e.g. Ofsted). They can then be included in your portfolio and linked to achieving your targets and planning.

## Practice suggestions

- Always date each document you write, including the year. It is so hard to remember when something happened for a child when you are writing a request in Year 5 or Year 9.

- Always put the version number of each document and link them to policies or connected processes.
- At the front of your portfolio always include your Action Planning and targets and also your establishment's development plan.
- Always include a flow chart or mapping of SEN provision and resources across the establishment's Provision Management chart.
- Always include a flow chart or list of the line management of roles and tasks across your establishment.
- Provide evidence of the latest national and local SEN data.
- Show budget planning and evidence of high needs spending as well as how the nominal SEN funding is being used.
- Include the SEN register.
- Include the SEN Calendar for the year.

If you work in this manner, you will then only have the last half-term's documentation at the very most to add if an inspection announcement is made. You will feel prepared and in control whatever stage of development you are at.

## 2.6 Well-being of staff

Being an advocate for the well-being of staff, including yourself, is vital. Times for thinking about well-being are when:

- a number of significant changes are happening;
- changes are being embedded (at least a year after the initial change);
- staff are required to assimilate a significant number of traumatic events or occurrences on a regular basis;
- a bereavement within the staff, the children or young people and the local community occurs;
- a change of role occurs;
- an inspection is due or has just occurred;
- and many more events could be added.

Consider what could be implemented or offered by your senior leadership team members to help staff cope with the many issues which occur. Professional supervision sessions might be applicable for middle or senior managers, while clinical supervision might be required for the people designated for safeguarding or looked after children. The timing of change needs to be carefully planned so that staff do not immediately feel overburdened and unsupported. If there is whole institutional disruption or distress, can you provide nurture through providing refreshments or lunch so that these essential, but often neglected aspects of life are managed by the leadership, giving staff the feeling of being valued and respected?

As SENCO, it might be that you will need to manage timetabling support with well-being kept in mind. Working on a 1:1 basis with a child with very complex needs, requiring physical stamina as well as educational skills can be very demanding and exhausting. Do such support staff and teachers get a chance to have a break and to re-charge their batteries? Such ways of working may seem to be expensive and time-consuming, but if members of staff go off sick due to stress or resign, then your workload as SENCO multiples overnight. Be proactive in thinking about all your staff's well-being and your own. This might mean that your calendar has to take into consideration when progress review meetings can be held so that teachers are not expected to analyse all their data and consider new strategies and interventions for children and young people with SEN, alongside writing annual reports. You may also need to include additional budgets for individual children's needs so that staff can attend training together or so that there can be additional time for planning or for handovers. Thinking about these things prior to implementation can ensure everyone is well prepared, budgets and requests for funding are realistic and everyone feels supported and valued. Providing such thought to well-being can prevent 'burn-out', low morale and a quick turnover of staff.

## What does this mean for the SENCO?

- *Reflect on your need for leadership training and mentoring and then ask for assistance if necessary.*
- *Ensure that you fit into your timetable opportunities to learn about employment regulations.*
- *Ensure that all paperwork actively demonstrates the inclusive ethos of your establishment and that it is clear to all that every child matters, including those with a special educational need.*
- *You will need to work closely with the other members of the management/senior leadership team to decide the annual calendar and the responsibilities and roles of all line managers throughout the organization.*
- *Do not underestimate the importance of administrative support.*
- *Do not forget about well-being as it can prevent unwanted surprises and additional expense.*

## Direct Links to the SEND Code of Practice

- 5.54 The role of the SENCO [in early years provision] involves:
  - advising and supporting colleagues . . .
- 5.56 Typically, the role of the Area SENCO includes:
  - supporting the development and delivery of training both for individual settings and on a wider basis.
- 6.87 The SENCO has an important role to play with the head teacher and governing body, in determining the strategic development of SEN policy and provision in the school. They will be most effective in that role if they are part of the school leadership team.
- 6.89 The SENCO provides professional guidance to colleagues . . .
- 7.22 Colleges . . . should ensure that there is a named person in the college with oversight of SEN provision . . .This person should contribute to the strategic and operational management of the college.

## Resources

1. This is a very useful autism Education Trust Sensory checklist: http://www.aettraininghubs.org.uk/wp-content/uploads/2012/05/37.2-Sensory-assessment-checklist.pdf (accessed 28 February 2016).
2. A Positive Environment Checklist. This is a checklist created by Leicestershire County Council which focuses especially on the environment and behaviour: http://www.leics.gov.uk/learning_environment_checklist_-_2007_version.pdf (accessed 28 February 2016).

# 3 The SENCO and whole school development

**Introduction**

This chapter will explain how you as the SENCO need to ensure that SEN is enshrined within all aspects of whole school planning and action and not just considered as an 'add-on' or in a separate manner. To help you to do this, the important elements of a SEN Information Report, the Local Offer and a SEN policy will be explored initially. As the SEN leader and manager of an establishment, you will also be responsible for providing the best possible resources and learning experiences for children or young people with special educational needs. This chapter will therefore also help you consider how to make financial and business development decisions within your settings, schools and colleges. You will be asked to consider how budgeting and also costing of time and equipment, especially with regards to Education, Health and Care (EHC) plans are carried out. The current focus on progress and outcomes rather than on 'provision' is considered here to show how it could impact on and influence how budgets are managed.

The next part of this chapter will then help you think about how you provide SEN initial or continuing professional development for all your staff. Finally, you will be introduced to how as SENCO you can carry out Action Research studies to inform practice and whole school development, working with colleagues to help increase understanding and skills.

## 3.1 The SEN Information Report, the Local Offer and the SEN Policy

### The SEN Information Report

There are no requirements for early years providers to produce a SEN Information Report, but they must:

> provide information for parents on how they support children with SEN and disabilities, and should regularly review and evaluate the quality and breadth of the support they offer or can access for children with SEN or disabilities.
>
> (DfE and DoH, 2015: 5.7: 80)

Local authorities are also responsible for making all early years providers aware that they should have regard to the SEND Code of Practice.

However, maintained nursery schools, like maintained schools and academies, must publish information on their website about the implementation of their

**Table 3.1** SEN Information Report Checklist

| *Required information* | *Fully* | *Mentioned* | *Not mentioned* |
|---|---|---|---|
| Areas of SEN need supported within the setting/ school<br>• High incident needs<br>• Low incident needs | | | |
| Names of policies which inform how SEN needs are assessed | | | |
| Names of policies which inform how the needs of children and young people with SEN are identified | | | |
| Name and contact details of the SENCO (maintained schools) | | | |
| How and when parents with children who have a special educational need are:<br>• consulted<br>• involved | | | |
| How and when young people with SEN are:<br>• consulted<br>• involved | | | |
| An explanation of the assessing and reviewing arrangements in place to evidence progress and achieving outcomes for all children and young people with SEN | | | |
| Clear information about how children and young people with SEN are helped to:<br>• move through transitions/phases of education<br>• prepare for adulthood | | | |
| An explanation about the establishment's approach to teaching children and young people with SEN | | | |
| Details about how children and young people with SEN are supported through:<br>• adaptations to the curriculum<br>• adaptations to the environment | | | |
| Details of staff SEN expertise and training | | | |
| Details of how specialist SEN expertise is secured | | | |
| An explanation of how provision for children and young people with SEN is evaluated | | | |
| Information about how children and young people with SEN are included and engaged in school activities | | | |

**Table 3.1** (continued)

| *Required information* | *Fully* | *Mentioned* | *Not mentioned* |
|---|---|---|---|
| Details of available pastoral support to help improve emotional and social development and prevent bullying | | | |
| Details of multi-professional working, support services and voluntary sector involvement focused on supporting the children and young people with SEN and their families | | | |
| Details of the arrangements in place to handle parental complaints about SEN provision | | | |

Source: Adapted from the SEND Code of Practice (DfE and DoH, 2015: 6.79: 106–7).

policy for children and young people with SEN. This is the responsibility of the governing bodies or proprietors. It is vital to remember that any changes to SEN provision or policy should be added to this report as soon as possible and that the SEN Information Report itself should be updated at least on an annual basis.

So what must a SEN Information Report include? Before looking at the checklist (Table 3.1) go to your current establishment's Information Report and identify what it includes and how it talks about SEN provision. Now look at what should be included as stated in the SEND Code of Practice (DfE and DoH, 2015: 6.79: 106).

It is also important to clearly say how the nursery, school or college contributes to the Local Offer, and to provide a direct link to the published Local Offer. Be as honest as you can about this and try to read your Information Report from the point of view of a young person with special educational needs or a parent without any SEN knowledge. Would you be able to understand how a child with special educational needs in your nursery or school would be supported to achieve their best? Would it be clear who to approach for help and what to ask for help with? Also identifying elements on this checklist which are either fully discussed, mentioned or omitted altogether can help you question and examine whether this is an area of provision which needs to be developed. Don't forget this SEN Information Report also allows you to CELEBRATE practice, so don't miss anything out.

There is no such direction for further education colleges with regards to the publication of SEN information.

## The Local Offer

When first mentioned, some local authorities thought that each school (SENCO) had to produce a 'Local Offer'. However, a Local Offer is a statutory duty of the local authorities to develop and publish and it is stated in the SEND Code of Practice that its development will help both education, social care and improve health provision (DfE and DoH, 2015: 4.3: 60). It must detail the provision a local authority 'expects' to be available across education, health and social care for all children and young people who have a special educational need and/or disability, both within its own area and outside of the local area. This is an important point for specific groups of children and young people who may also have a SEN and/or disability such as looked after children or young people in Pupil Referral Units (PRU). There is a common framework for the Local Offer provided by the Special Educational Needs and Disability Regulations 2014 which all local authorities must meet (DfE and DoH, 2015: 4.30: 66–7). As a SENCO, it will be useful to remember the five key elements that every Local Offer should comprise. These are:

- collaborative
- accessible
- comprehensive
- up to date
- transparent.

So what do SENCOs need to know or do about the Local Offer? When talking about the involvement of schools, colleges, health services and others with the Local Offer, the SEND Code of Practice (DfE and DoH, 2015: 4.14: 63) says they must *co-operate* with each other. This requirement includes maintained school, academies, free schools, further education colleges, sixth form colleges and PRUs. Interestingly 'proprietors of independent specialist colleges and independent schools specially organised to make provision for children and young people with SEN' (given approval by the Secretary of State) 'for the purpose of enabling parents and young people to request that they are named on an EHC plan' (DfE and DoH, 2015: 4.15: 64) must also co-operate.

In relation to early years education providers, a local authority should *engage* with them about the Local Offer. However, maintained nursery schools and relevant early education providers must co-operate (DfE and DoH, 2015: 5.7: 80).

## The SEN policy

In the past, the SEN policy, like many other policies, I suspect, has all too frequently been written by one teacher (usually the SENCO) in isolation, adopted by the governing body/trustees and then gathered dust in a cupboard. Of course, this is not what a policy is for; it should be a working document which informs practice and supports the development of the whole school plan. It should at the very least be reviewed annually and updated in between times as frequently as necessary. It should also be accessible to parents, carers and young people, thus jargon should be avoided or at least clearly explained.

It is for these reasons, I would suggest, that the SEND Code of Practice (DfE and DoH, 2015) now makes direct links between the SEN policy and daily practice. It says, for example, that maintained nursery schools must write a report about the *implementation* of their SEN policy and it indicates that one of the roles of SENCOs in schools will probably be carrying out the *daily operation* of the SEN policy. By doing this, it not only makes it clear that the policy must accurately reflect daily practice, but that the writing and reviewing of the SEN policy are not the responsibility of the SENCO or SEN lead, but the governing body's or the proprietors' role. In reality, of course, it is frequently the SENCO who gets the task to actually lead the writing of the policy, but this should be completed in collaboration with other members of staff, the SEN governors, parents and carers and pupils. In fact, I would say that this joint approach to writing and reviewing the policy is a must because it is now essential that you can evidence how parental and pupil views are incorporated into policies, as well as demonstrating how all your policies link together to inform school development and action.

It is therefore not surprising that some local authorities are advising that the SEN Information Report should form the majority of the SEN policy to prevent the duplication of tasks and save time and energy. By just putting an introduction about the context and overall values of your establishment and additional details such as dates for review, in the SEN Information Report, (as detailed in the SEN Information Report Checklist above), you will have created a policy that fulfils all the current requirements.

**Practice suggestions**

- Always put the SEN policy monitoring and review process into your annual calendar of important events. This will ensure the Information Report is regularly reviewed and updated and will also enable you to plan for meetings you will need to collect the views of all your stakeholders.
- Avoid jargon and the use of acronyms throughout both the policy and Information Report. Use sub-headings that are completely transparent to every reader. For example, instead of saying, 'Definitions of SEND', why not just say 'What is special educational needs (SEN) and disability?'
- Ensure that when you review the SEN policy, you also have other relevant policies alongside, so that you can evidence that there is a strategic approach to SEND.
- Make sure that what you put in the policy does actually occur in practice. Use appendices to include important information such as flow charts detailing school assessment and progress processes and timeframes, and line management responsibilities for SEN. If these are stated and actually happen, this produces external and internal confidence in the leadership team's expertise. As SENCO, you need to show that SEN is very central to the leadership's strategic plans.
- Never say that you will review the SEN policy on your own. Remember this should be completed in collaboration with as many colleagues, parents/carers, governors, and young people as possible.

## 3.2 Financial and business development

The SENCO budget and the overall financial responsibility for how funds relating to SEN are spent have over the past few years grown as the need to evidence 'value for money' has become a key focus at the national, local and individual establishment level. As is the same for many other aspects of the SENCO role and responsibilities, this is nothing new, but just given greater emphasis in this current

SEND Code of Practice. So often in the past when I spoke to SENCOs, they did not know what the SEN budget was or how it was spent. Fortunately, this is changing, but it does mean that SENCOs now need to have a good understanding of business and financial planning. So what do we mean by 'value for money' and how can you as a SENCO ensure this is being delivered for the children or young people you work with and for your establishment?

### Value for money

In 2004, the DCSF described value for money in the following way. 'Value for money means delivering the best outcomes from a given set of resources'. http://webarchive.nationalarchives.gov.uk/20100202100434/http://www.standards.dcsf.gov.uk/vfm/downloads/PDF/strategicplanning.pdf (accessed 5 March 2016). It continues by using 'three Es' to explain the key elements of value for money in a way I think is very helpful to you as a SENCO today.

- *Economy*: securing goods, services and personnel at the best price for a given level of quality and at the lowest cost.
- *Efficiency*: the best deployment of those goods, services and personnel to achieve a set of outputs.
- *Effectiveness:* the right mixture of outputs to achieve a particular set of outcomes. See http://webarchive.nationalarchives.gov.uk/20100202100434/http://www.standards.dcsf.gov.uk/vfm/downloads/PDF/strategicplanning.pdf (page 3) (accessed 5 March 2016).

It is also important here to remember that these three Es are most effective when they are well balanced – 'relatively low-cost/economy, high-efficiency/productivity and successful outcomes/effectiveness' (Anthony, 2010: 95). Anthony (2010: 94) continues:

> Fundamentally 'value for money' means delivering the best outcomes from a given set of resources with a limited income . . . The SENCO must always aim to ensure that funding is spent wisely and targeted to improve standards; and the new Labour government in its 'Value for Money' guidance material clarified this even more: 'Improving value for money in schools means improving the way schools allocate and use their resources in order to improve children's outcomes in a continuous and sustainable way', see http://webarchive.nationalarchives.gov.uk/20100202101002/standards.dcsf.gov.uk/vfm/ (accessed 5 March 2016).

The language used, 'outcomes', 'targeted' and 'improve standards' is of course very familiar to you today. Thus, during the last decade, processes and systems have been developing to help SENCOs manage this aspect of the role as effectively as possible. When considering what the three Es mean for SEN non-human resources, the first two, economy and efficiency, can be managed effectively in the same manner as any other resource in an educational environment. Table 3.2 provides basic guidance when considering new expenditure on new interventions or assessments.

**Table 3.2** Guidance when purchasing SEN non-human resources

| *Tasks* | *Key considerations* |
|---|---|
| Expenditure | • Identify the need for the new resource/get three quotes if appropriate<br>• How many children/young people (or staff) will benefit from it?<br>• Does it support a high or low incident need?<br>• Which funding stream will this be taken from?<br>• Does it actually support other groups (e.g. pupil premium)?<br>• Is it sustainable or need annual additional training costs?<br>• Ensure you keep within the approved budget |
| Ordering | • Order from reputable firms only<br>• Are you able to see a sample/example before you purchase?<br>• Can you purchase it on a trial basis first?<br>• How many members of staff have been involved in making the decision about this new resource?<br>• If a new intervention/scheme, have you checked it has been well developed or that there is a sound evidence base?<br>• Order in liaison with bursar/business director – ensure other factors such as health and safety are also considered prior to ordering<br>• Check order information, e.g. time for delivery, and guarantee period |
| Management of resource | • Immediately put on your list of resources (SEN Information Report) with linked costs or purchase price with any additional costs which might need to be added to costings for EHC plans and high needs funding<br>• Identify depreciation rate/years before it needs to be replaced (estimate)<br>• Locate resources for efficiency of use<br>• Is this resource going to be shared between establishments? If so, details on how, when and who all need to be agreed<br>• Identify children or young people who will be using this resource<br>• Plan training/introduction for staff who will be using this resource<br>• Identify who will monitor the new resource – use and condition |
| Resources (additional costs/ requirements) Monitoring and evaluation | • Storage – new boxes required/ease of access<br>• Ensure any relevant training is accessed quickly<br>• Ensure you add to budget any possible repair/upkeep costs<br>• Identify staff who will be responsible for monitoring:<br>  • its use<br>  • its durability<br>  • whether it meets the identified need(s) for children or young people<br>  • its impact on learning and outcomes<br>  • its value for money<br>• Determine a date when the new resource will be evaluated by the establishment or class or an individual<br>• Record all of this in your evidence of budget management |

Also whenever possible, do try to compare two or three similar products just as you would when you purchase a new car or a holiday. You will need to ask different questions for various types of resources. The following case study will help you think about the areas you may need to consider.

## Case study 3.1 Resources

College A wanted to purchase a new on-line spelling program. In order to ensure that the selected program could support as many students for as long as possible the SEN lead identified three possible options and measured each one in the following ways (Table 3.3).

**Table 3.3** Comparison of resources

| *Areas for consideration* | *Resource 1* | *Resource 2* | *Resource 3* |
| --- | --- | --- | --- |
| Who? | Limited to basic vocabulary | Three levels of difficulty | Six levels of difficulty |
| Cost? | Purchase cost £600<br>Site licence £150<br>Annual upgrade costs not known – but will be applicable | Purchase cost £500<br>No site licence<br>No upgrade provision mentioned | Purchase cost £700<br>Site licence (one cost to cover all site) £300<br>Free annual upgrade |
| Staffing implications? | Teacher control options included | Teacher would need to constantly support students as usage instructions are complex | Teacher control options included<br>Easy to follow instructions<br>No additional staff training required |
| Appropriateness? | Format not suitable for students at college | Format not suitable for students at college | Other SENCOs have recommended<br>Motivating challenges<br>Appropriate format for students aged 16+ |
| Ease of usage? | Limited | Not suitable | Formative assessments automatically saved in tutor/teacher area |
| Purpose? | Only pre-programmed words available<br>Methods – too similar to school experiences | Bland and repetitive tasks/methods of teaching<br>Limited purpose | Progress charts for each student available<br>Multi-sensory<br>Progress charts/assessment record available |
| Trial period? | Yes – 2 weeks | Yes – 1 month | Yes – 3 months |

### Decision

In consultation with other members of the senior leadership, including the business manager/bursar, it was agreed that Resource 3 would be most effective for:

- the greatest number of students with special educational needs;
- staffing implications;
- on-going costs;
- support with assessing student outcomes.

The information provided in Table 3.2 can be adapted or enhanced depending on the specific needs of your provision, school or college. The case study also illustrates how comparing similar products can be advantageous. From this section of the chapter you can see how careful you have to be when ordering new resources. A quick, unconsidered purchase can have long-term impact on children's and young people's outcomes, your whole school SEN effectiveness and on the SEN budget!

The final, but definitely most expensive resource is your staff. In recent years, findings from some research (Symes and Humphrey, 2011) has found that the use of teaching assistants does not always ensure that pupils make progress. However, when reviewed carefully, it is not that all use of teaching assistants is ineffective, but that it is how they are used that is most important. As discussed in Chapter 2, Section 2.3, identifying the skills and knowledge of staff is crucial to whom you employ and for which role. Not unexpectedly, educational establishments and especially schools responded to these research findings in different ways. Some schools decided to employ a few more teachers and to stop employing teaching assistants, whereas others reconsidered the skills of the staff they employed. For example, many schools and colleges now only employ graduates as teaching assistants, learning mentors or pastoral support workers. Inexplicitly linked to the initial employment of staff is the on-going skilling-up of staff. This was discussed in detail in Chapter 2, but must again be considered when thinking about financial planning, as this will be an on-going expense which must be part of the whole provision, school or college planning. Using your audit of staff skills and the needs of the children or young people with special educational needs, as well as all children or young people, will help you cost the immediate, intermediate and long-term staffing needs. As with all other strategic leadership roles of the SENCO, the use of the funding requested and received, specifically for children or young people with SEN, should be considered as part of the whole establishment's provision. How, for whom and why funds are used must be advantageous to the progress and to the achievement of all children or young people and this needs to be evidenced through the establishment's data and from qualitative stakeholder feedback. As stated in the SEND Code of Practice (DfE and DoH, 2015: 6.97: 110):

> The SENCO, headteacher and governing body or proprietor should establish a clear picture of the resources that are available to the school. They should consider their strategic approach to meeting SEN in the context of the total resources available.

How funding for SEN is distributed is undergoing what appears to be continuous adjustment and varies from local authority to local authority. Therefore, as SENCO, you must first of all understand what the SEND Code of Practice (DfE and DoH, 2015) says, so that you can relate it to your own establishment with regards to funding and then it is essential that you attend local training and update sessions with regards to budgets and access to additional sources of funding. Table 3.4 provides guidance on funding for nursery schools, schools and colleges.

**Table 3.4** Funding guidance from the SEND Code of Practice

| *Type of provision* | *Funding information* |
|---|---|
| Early years | • All providers with funded early years places must meet the needs of children with SEN and/or disabilities<br>• Your local authority must ensure the funding arrangements enable suitable support for children with SEN and/or disabilities to be provided |
| Schools | • Ensure you know the way in which your local funding formula is decided (schools and academies)<br>• Sixth forms (school and academy) are allocated funds from a national funding formula<br>• Within your school's overall budget there is a notional SEN budget. This is not ring-fenced.<br>• There is additional top-up funding for SEN provision which exceeds the national prescribed threshold |
| Further education | • Additional funding for students with SEN is provided. This is not ring-fenced and is included in their main allocation<br>• There is additional top-up funding for SEN provision which exceeds the national prescribed threshold<br>*NOTE: Colleges are funded in the following ways:*<br>• The Education Funding Agency (EFA) funds all 16–18-year-olds and those (with support from home local authorities) with an EHC plan aged between 19 and 25<br>• The Skills Funding Agency (SFA) funds all students aged 19 or above, except those with an EHC plan |

(DfE and DoH, 2015)

## 3.3 Continuing professional development

This section of the chapter will focus on helping you as a SENCO identify what types of continuing professional development (CPD) your whole staff need to ensure they can help all the children or young people with special educational needs. Remember CPD might not be on specific areas of need, but could be more generic, such as understanding child development or phonics, and as such should be planned in consultation with a senior colleague in charge of literacy or pastoral support. This is where whole school development planning is essential.

There are many ways to provide professional development, but at all times you should keep the targets as stated in the whole school development plan in focus, with particular sight on those relating to SEN. Continuing professional development can be achieved through a variety of methods and is not just limited to external courses, accredited programmes or face-to-face training. There should be a blend of approaches which, while they may overlap, do have a specific objective. All education staff are extremely busy and so how you enhance their skills and knowledge about SEN needs to always be linked to children's learning and to enhance their professional practice. The following questions will help you think about how you begin to draw up a long-term action plan for staff development.

**Practice questions**

- How do you use the audit of staff expertise to help you design a continuing professional development (CPD) plan?
- How does your plan of action differ/remain similar for the different professionals working within your establishment? Do you have a 'fair' way of determining who receives funding or additional study time?
- Do you plan all CPD around the establishment's development plan, especially in relation to SEN?
- Do you take years of service into account, as well as other factors such as performance management achievements and sick leave?

A SENCO needs to have an overarching strategic approach to CPD because many either subject- or age-specific training or academic study programmes can enhance the teaching and learning of children and young people with SEN, as well as for all others. Thus, it might be helpful to use the headings universal, targeted and specialist for CPD as you do for SEN provision. Look at the suggestions below and see what type of approaches and programmes you already use and for whom. Then see if you could enhance the coverage and impact of the SEN CPD your establishment offers to: support staff, facility and business staff, teachers, SEN staff, senior leaders and other professions. This may only require an additional sentence or change of emphasis as part of a peer observation proforma, or may require actual significant changes such as modelling practice with a particular focus on working with children or young people, for example, with a speech, language and communication need (SLCN) or setting aside a significant budget for training in specific new programmes or interventions such as the introduction of visual timetables using Widgit symbols http://www.widgit.com/ (accessed 5 March 2016) or video interaction guidance (VIG) http://www.videointeractionguidance.net/ (accessed 5 March 2016).

### Universal approaches

- Peer mentoring/peer observations
- Team teaching
- Modelling
- Case study reviews and reflections (useful for multi-professional teams)
- On-line training, e.g. safeguarding, health and safety, SEN awareness raising needs focused on the four areas of need
- Whole school subject/curriculum/developmental INSET training
- Work moderation (within and between establishments)
- Staff meeting short input sessions
- 'SEN' fact of the week on noticeboards or via email/intranet
- SEN information sheets in staff areas or on staff development intranet space
- Introduction of a whole school new practice, e.g. handwriting or visual systems

### Targeted approaches

- Specific within establishment input for different professionals working within the educational establishment, e.g. 'understanding behaviour' for lunch time supervisors or 'provision mapping' for teaching staff.
- Specific external or on-line training on a specific area of SEN at an undergraduate level to provide confidence and knowledge to an identified number of support staff.
- SEN research projects focused on an area of need which will give middle managers the opportunity to lead an evaluation which might lead to a whole school change of practice or individual professional development.
- Team teaching targeted to enhance specific teachers' skills.
- Planning and business development for teaching staff/SENCO working with business/HR colleagues.
- Year group, subject teachers or specific group of teaching staff – specific input to improve outcomes for all children or young people, including those with SEN, e.g. http://www.canterbury.ac.uk/education/our-work/research-knowledge-exchange/teaching-and-learning-academy/regional-centres.aspx(accessed 5 March 2016).

### Specialist approaches

- Individual qualifications to provide specific SEN leaders within your establishment, e.g. Foundation degree in SEN (support staff); MA in Special Needs and Inclusion/areas of SEN for teachers or other professionals; Ed.D or PhD in SEN for leaders.
- Individual approaches for additional expertise, e.g. SLCN specialist support or coaching and mentoring, supervision or counselling.

In this way, a whole-establishment approach towards professional development can be planned across a three-to-five-year period and the budget can be connected, appropriately enabling SEN knowledge and skills to be constantly improving, using a coherent approach which can be carefully mapped and evaluated within the development plan. Working in this way will also support and interlock with performance management processes and the specialist expertise needed to provide high quality education for children or young people with complex needs.

## 3.4 Embedding evidence-based practice

Gone are the days when practitioners were just expected to implement programmes that others had developed. All practitioners and especially SENCOs are now expected to actively enable and cultivate critical enquiry, review and reflection through the evidence-based practice process. The SEND Code of Practice (DfE and DoH, 2015: 6.62: 103) says that for children and young people identified as having a special educational need, the SENCO, class teacher and specialists 'should consider a range of evidence-based and effective teaching approaches . . . in order to support the child's progress'. It is argued that it is essential that the key principles of evidence-based practice are embedded in our education establishments to provide practitioners with the skills to rigorously critically review and reflect on the impact of changes. This is considered especially important for those working with our children, young people and families with special educational needs. From its medical origins, evidence-based practice is now embedded at all levels of the education system, from the development of national government policy through to individual school-based research and evidence.

Within a single educational institution, evidence-based practice might be achieved by:

- collectively critically reflecting on national or even international research;
- working and talking to other similar educational establishments about specific interventions or changes to practice;
- ensuring all interventions are monitored, reviewed and the impact evaluated;
- carrying out action research which is school-based (Ekins, 2012).

### Action research

Cohen, Manion and Morrison (2007: 297) state: 'action research is a powerful tool for change and improvement at the local level' and that its scope 'as a method is impressive'. There are many ways to define what action research is, but for our purpose here Kemmis and McTaggart's (1992: 10) definition is perhaps the most useful: 'To do action research is to plan, act, observe and reflect more carefully, more systematically, and more rigorously than one usually does in everyday life.'

Action research is seen as a way of empowering teachers and of ensuring that research impacts directly on practice, although of course it is not without its critics. When completing the National Award for SEN Co-ordination, you may be asked to carry out a piece of action research, enabling you to see how such a method can help you evidence your reasons for changing practice and/or implementing something new. There are many different models of action research. A simple model might look like this:

1. Identify an aspect of practice in your provision, school or college you know needs evaluation or improvement.
2. Use research and other literature to help you decide a way forward.
3. Decide how you are going to implement this and action it.
4. Analyse and evaluate what happens.
5. Modify the plan if necessary and once again analyse and evaluate what happens.
6. Repeat this cycle as many times as is necessary to achieve the result you want.

Whichever model of action research you adopt, ensure that as a matter of priority you always carefully consider the ethical issues for all participants involved, whether children, young people or adults. Respect, confidentiality and anonymity are all vital aspects to consider when carrying out an action research project.

## 3.5 SEN knowledge (areas of need)

The four broad areas of need are described in the SEND Code of Practice (DfE and DoH, 2015: 5.32, 6.28–6.35, 7.22) as:

- Communication and interaction (6.28)
- Cognition and learning (6.30)
- Social, emotional and mental health difficulties (6.32)
- Sensory and/or physical need (6.34).

SENCOs are not expected to be the 'experts' or have the 'specialist' knowledge about the areas of need. Although the same language used in the current Code of Practice is found in the original version, the actuality and school expectations were very different. In 1994, the SENCO was expected to be the 'font of all knowledge' about SEN and so this has been a significant shift for more experienced SENCOs. The current SEND Code of Practice (DfE and DoH, 2015: 5.15, 6.25, 7.22), however, clearly says that it is the early years' providers, schools or colleges as a whole and not the SENCO alone, that 'should review how well equipped they are to provide support across these [broad] areas'. Thus, all aspects of a SENCO's role reinforces the importance and expectations of a whole school approach to supporting and providing high quality education to children or young people with special educational needs through high quality differentiated teaching, and targeted short-term interventions. Only if the children or young people continue to make little or no progress 'despite evidence-based SEN support delivered by appropriately trained staff' (DfE and DoH, 2015: 6.59: 102) should external specialists be involved. As the SENCO you will be expected to identify the specialist expertise required from your SEN Information Report or the Local Offer and in partnership with other professionals and parents arrange for the assessment, support or intervention to begin as quickly as possible. This may require direct commissioning of specific services when there is no other available local authority or health service provision. This of course could have an impact on budgets and resource planning, including staff training. Depending on local need, this also might influence the decision of the governing body or management board over the medium term to employ certain specialists directly, such as speech and language therapists or educational psychologists.

Nevertheless, I would still argue that for many SENCOs a sound and enhanced knowledge about areas of special educational needs can be extremely beneficial when arranging for the assessment, provision and targeted outcomes for children or young people, as well as the SEN strategic direction for either an early years provision, a school or a college.

### What does this mean for the SENCO?

- *Work with colleagues to ensure that the SEN Information Report is agreed and known by all the staff, governors, parents and children/young people.*
- *Ensure that you attend local authority networking opportunities so that you can influence or at least liaise about items on the Local Offer.*

- *Liaise with your establishment's finance director or bursar and obtain finance training if necessary so that you can ensure all SEN provision provides 'value for money'.*
- *Work with senior leaders to plan expenditure for all aspects of SEN needs within a three- or five-year plan for the whole establishment.*
- *Secure an effective and well-managed continuing professional development (CPD) action plan through careful mapping of SEN, staff expertise, and whole school training needs.*
- *Consider how evidence-based practice is used to critically reflect on provision and impact, at the national, local and individual establishment levels.*
- *Identify a piece of action research you could lead with colleagues.*
- *Determine what CPD you most need to enable you to fulfil the SENCO roles and responsibilities.*

## Direct Links to the SEND Code of Practice

- 5.20 Early years providers and educational settings should have arrangements in place that include a clear approach to assessing SEN. This should be part of the setting's overall approach to monitoring the progress and development of all children.
- 6.3 School leaders should regularly review how expertise and resources used to address SEN can be used to build the quality of whole school provision as part of their approach to school improvement.
- 6.4 The quality of teaching for pupils with SEN, and the progress made by pupils, should be a core part of the school's performance management arrangements and its approach to professional development for all teaching and support staff.
- 6.5 The identification of SEN should be built into the overall approach to monitoring the progress and development of all pupils.
- 6.17 Class and subject teachers, supported by the senior leadership team, should make regular assessments of progress for all pupils. These should seek to identify pupils making less than expected progress given their age and individual circumstances.
- 7.4 Colleges should offer an inclusive approach to learning and teaching, with high quality teaching which is differentiated for individuals. This approach should be embedded in their provision in all subject areas and at all levels, and support the teaching of all students, including those with SEN.
- 7.23 Specialist help should be involved where the student's needs are not being met by the strong, evidence-based support provided by the college.

## Resources

- Visual support Widgit symbols: http://www.widgit.com/ (accessed 5 March 2016)
- Video interaction guidance (VIG): http://www.videointeractionguidance.net/ (accessed 5 March 2016).

# 4 The co-ordination of provision

**Introduction**

Chapter 4 commences with the identification of the SEN areas of need as detailed in the SEND Code of Practice (DfE and DoH, 2015). Carrying forward discussions from Chapters 2 and 3 about the importance of impact and outcomes and how this needs to influence business and financial decisions, the focus on individual children's or young people's special educational needs will be explored. This leads on to how SENCOs might consider how to organize and manage the identification and assessment of need within their own educational setting within the national framework of SEN support (the Graduated Approach) and Education, Health and Care (EHC) plans. The monitoring and evaluation of interventions and quality first teaching provision will also be part of this discussion, paying particular attention to how impact and outcomes can be measured. At the end of this chapter you will be given some ideas to help you ensure that your establishment really considers the impact that transitions can have, providing a holistic view of why they can make so much difference to progress and well-being for all children and young people, but particularly those with a special educational need.

## 4.1 Identification and assessment of needs

### Special educational needs and disability

> The Foreword of the SEND Code of Practice introduced in 2014 clearly voices Parliament's view that all children and young people including those with special educational needs and disabilities is that they achieve well in their early years, at school and in college, and lead happy and fulfilled lives.
>
> (DfE and DoH, 2015: 11)

As a SENCO or named person for SEN you will passionately agree with this statement and will strive to achieve it for all the children and young people learning at your establishment. Where in the past this has often felt like a lonely ambition and task for the SENCO, the current SEND Code of Practice clearly articulates and enforces the fact that the achievement of children and young people with special educational needs and disabilities is everyone's responsibility. As previously mentioned, all teachers are now accountable as well as responsible for the progress and development of all children and young people in their class. It also ensures that teachers are aware that this includes time when the children and young people with special educational needs and disabilities are with other specialists. This sentence alone, I believe, really illustrates the commitment of this Code of Practice to close some of the loopholes with regards to the responsibility about the achievement and life chances of children and young people with special educational needs and disabilities. It is no longer encouraging the on-going development of inclusive practice, but telling professionals (health, education and social care) that they are required to work in this way. Thus although the definitions of special educational needs (SEN) (see Appendix 1 in this book) and the legal obligations of the Equality Act 2010 (see Appendix 2 in this book) have only been tweaked, it is their enactment that has been strengthened.

**Practice questions**

- How many of the staff and children or young people in your establishment know the definitions (generally) of SEN and disability?
- Do all your staff support the strengthening of their responsibility and accountability for all the children or young people they teach? If not, why not?
- Does your ethos or vision statement support this understanding and is it reinforced not only in policy but practice as well?
- Do your reward and recommendation systems recognise the progress and development of children or young people with special educational needs or disabilities?
- Take a look at your response as an establishment to the Equality Act 2010. Is it robust enough? How frequently do you undertake 'learning walks' which focus on the environment (physical and sensory) for children and young people with SEN or disabilities? Is your accessibility plan current and also anticipatory? Does your budget allow for changes to the physical environment year on year and for additional auxiliary aids?
- Do you have a visual presence around the school celebrating equality of opportunity and difference?

### Areas of SEN

As explored in Chapter 3 (Section 3.5), the SEND Code of Practice identifies four areas of broad needs for schools and colleges. However, it is vital to understand that for all provisions, including early years, there is clear direction about ensuring the approach you decide upon in assessing whether SEN is part of an establishment's 'overall approach to monitoring the progress and development of all children' (DfE and DoH, 2015: 5.20: 82) – a system for all, enacted by all!

#### *Progress check at age 2*

Parents of children between the ages of 2 and 3 must receive a written summary of their child's progress which highlights their strengths as well as where progress is slower than expected or where there are significant concerns (DfE and DoH, 2015: 5.23: 83). The areas practitioners have to focus on for this review are:

- communication and language;
- physical development;
- personal, social and emotional development.

### *Early years*

Of course, progress and development are reviewed continually throughout the early years by practitioners, with the Early Years Foundation Stage (EYFS) profile usually completed in the final term of the year in which the children turn 5. This provides a 'well-rounded picture of a child's knowledge, understanding and abilities' (DfE and DoH, 2015: 5.26: 84) which should be able to inform plans for any additional SEN support.

### *The four broad areas of need for all practitioners and professionals*

Early years practitioners are, like all other professionals working in schools or colleges, asked to match a child's identified SEN within one of the following areas:

- communication and interaction;
- cognition and learning;
- social, emotional and mental health;
- sensory and/or physical needs.

### *Identifying need before making the decision that a child or young person has a special educational need*

This is a part of a SENCO's strategic leadership role which is most crucial wherever you are working. This is where you will know how effective and efficient you are being as a SENCO in fulfilling your roles and responsibilities. It is also the aspect of your role where the operational merges (hopefully seamlessly) with the strategic. It is what education establishments do at this point that I think enables inspectors, parents and carers, and the children and young people themselves, to identify:

- the true values and beliefs of an early years, a school or college establishment;
- the commitment of its staff (including governors or trustees) to developing inclusive practice;
- whether there are whole provision/school/college systems and processes in place for all children and young people, including those with SEN;
- the collaborative working of the senior leadership team and the role of the SENCO within this.

I say these things because if an educational establishment tries to support all of its children and young people positively, using a range of strategies and teaching methods at the universal and even targeted levels, the need for specialist SEN support should become less. Not only should this positively impact on academic progress and achievement, but it should also be reflected in the children and young people's self-esteem, sense of well-being and thus on their confidence and availability to take risks and have a go! As a teacher and a SENCO, do you find the best moment is when a child or young person makes a positive step forward, initially quite cautiously, but then 'with both feet'? Doesn't the determination on their faces, and the pride in themselves make you convinced you are in the 'right' role?

## Universal strategies and resources

So before we move on to examine SEN support, let's look at what can be included in your everyday provision for the use and benefit of all children and young people. Figure 4.1 illustrates a few universal strategies and resources you can introduce to enable and support all children and young people, including those with SEN. Some of the suggestions listed will of course not be appropriate for the age group you are working with, but I suspect you will be able to replace this item with

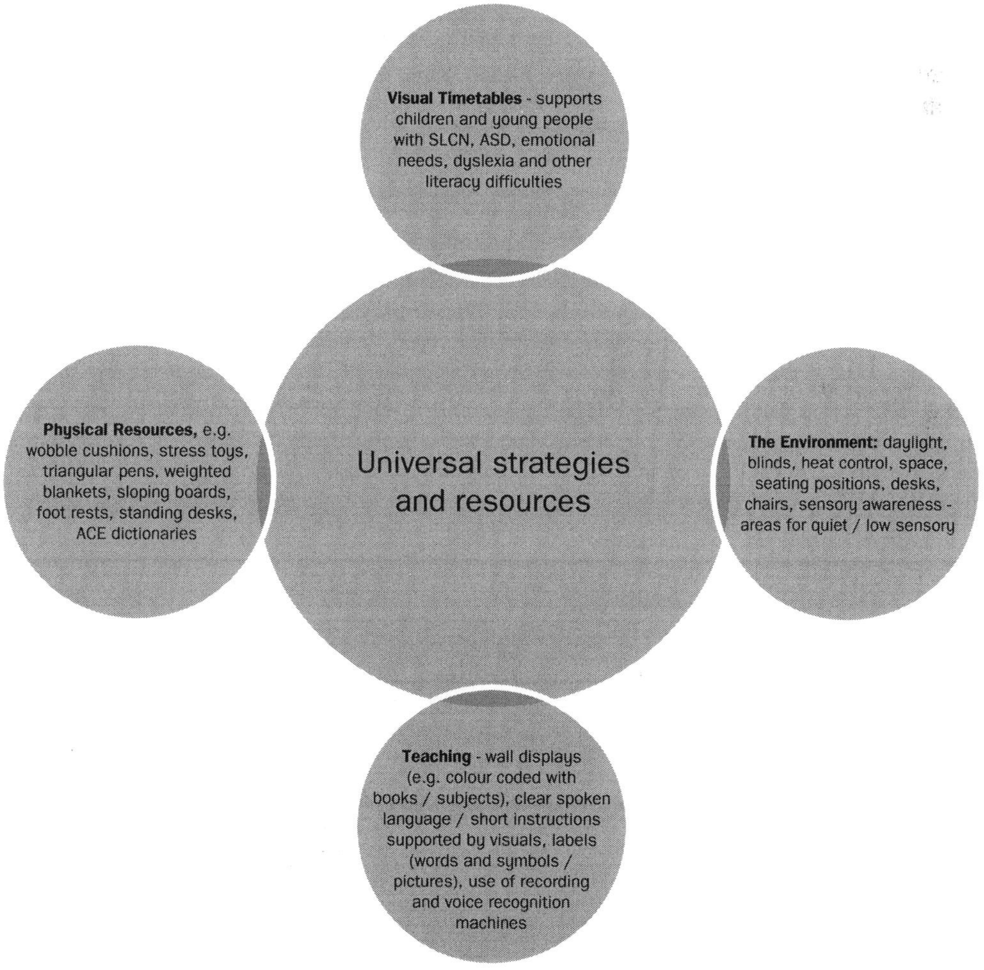


**Figure 4.1** Universal ways to support children's and young people's learning in a classroom prior to SEN identification

something more age-appropriate. Below are a couple of case studies which will help you think how you use your own resources. Some colleagues will undoubtedly say that with such options there will be arguments about who should have what and when, but with a variety of options (e.g. different-sized desks, foot rests and cushions) and positive modelling from the adults, they will soon become just part of the everyday equipment which is useful sometimes, but not all of the time.

### Case study 4.1 Reception class

In one school during the progress review meeting with the SENCO, a teacher discussed the difficulties she was having in helping the children in her reception class to sit still at their desks and on the floor. When an observation was carried out, it was found that the majority of the children were not able to touch the ground with their feet when they were sitting on their chairs, making the position for writing extremely uncomfortable. Also the area of the floor where they sat for stories and instructions was in the direct line of the door, resulting in a great draught, and the area itself was very small, meaning that the children had to sit cross-legged and extremely close to each other.

The issues identified were:

- The school could not afford new furniture.
- Furniture could not be moved to allow more space for the floor time activities.

The solutions identified were:

- Cushions, including a couple of wobble cushions, were purchased and placed in a box in the corner of the room for all children to use when necessary.
- Chairs and desks from different classrooms were shared around so that each room had a number of different sizes (and perhaps even colours).
- Sloping boards, foot rests (made out of wood or even old telephone directories or catalogues) and weighted blankets became resources to be used when required.
- Draught protection was put at the bottom of the door.
- Some of the children were allowed to sit on their chairs during floor time, allowing others to stretch out their legs.

### Case study 4.2 Using recording devices

One teacher had recognized that working memory was difficult for a number of students in a Year 9 class. The traditional visual supports did not appear to be enabling these students to work as independently as they needed to as they were heading towards examinations and preparation for employment. She noticed that these students (of a wide range of abilities) kept asking her to repeat the instructions (despite visual instructions being available). She had chunked her instructions and provided individual visual instruction sheets, but there were still a few students who could not successfully complete their work independently. She had noticed that these students immediately repeated her instructions aloud to themselves and so, taking the cue from them, she introduced a few recording devices to her universal resource list. She (or an ICT technician or support staff member) would record the instructions onto these devices for the lessons and then if students felt they needed to hear the instructions repeated, they would use these machines. Again after the first few lessons the initial fascination died down and they were used appropriately by those who needed them. This encouraged appropriate reinforcement, a strategy to support learning and personal independence.

### Targeted strategies and resources

For some children and young people, universal resources and strategies are not sufficient to enable them to make progress and develop in line with expected outcomes all of the time. Perhaps while evaluating the class provision map, the teacher or tutor notices that a child or young person is not making adequate progress in one aspect of their learning, but after discussing it with you, there is a feeling that this might not be a long-term difficulty or caused by a specific incident or external factor. At this point the professionals involved (including the parents/carers) must act immediately. At the progress review meeting, it is decided that further assessment and a targeted, short intervention will be undertaken to see if this can provide the necessary support to enable progress to continue. This is where you need to be able to co-ordinate provision to enable this short-term targeted intervention, whether it be additional phonic sessions or social understanding sessions, as quickly as possible. Because it is targeted support, the class/subject teacher might take the responsibility for this, managing the sessions with or without a learning mentor or teaching assistant and reporting back at the next progress review meeting whether it has been effective. To enable this type of proactive response to a learning need will require you to have considered factors such as how you are going to evidence whether the intervention is effective (as it might not be academic), e.g. through targeted intervention sheets. Also have you got the additional resources that may be required, flexibility with your support staff, appropriate assessment and even physical space? As it is targeted intervention, you, the SENCO, should be working with the teachers to ensure that they, with your support, can respond to this type of short-term support effectively and efficiently.

Above we have talked about how whole school systems and processes can quickly identify and support short-term learning difficulties such as provision maps and progress review meetings (see Section 4.3). Through these strategies and processes teachers and support staff are empowered to respond with your help and strategic leadership.

Therefore, to summarize, as a SENCO you will have, in collaboration with the other members of the leadership team, supported the introduction and implementation of processes, such as provision mapping and progress review meetings for all children and young people. You will have also looked at the whole establishment's resourcing and universal teaching strategies. It is important that this includes:

- assessments that teachers or tutors can carry out (considering time and skills required);
- training where necessary;
- an audit of all the equipment you have available;
- flexible staffing;
- intervention and evaluation template sheets;
- on-going involvement and consultation with parents/carers (and where possible the children and young people);
- external specialist assessment when necessary.

Speed, collaboration and consultation are significant areas to manage when considering additional support and as SENCO you will be vital in ensuring that the administrative, managerial and expertise elements of this process work together for the benefit of the children, young people and families. In these ways you are providing teachers, other senior leaders and support staff with the means to really 'own' their classes' progress and act immediately when this is not as expected.

Of course there will be the need to acknowledge that some children and young people require longer-term and more intense SEN support. It is at this point that a child or young person is identified as having a special educational need and is placed on the SEN register. This of course must be done with the parents' agreement.

## 4.2 Processes and systems: SEN support (the Graduated Approach) and Education, Health and Care (EHC) plans

A general SEN support term has replaced the previous SEN Action and SEN Action Plus stages of SEN identification. This was a strategic decision by the government to manoeuvre practice away from a focus on provision and funding to that of individual need, impact and outcomes. It is a personalized, cyclical process which encourages and enables an educational establishment to reflect on their practice, engage with other professionals and parents, and develop their skills and knowledge. The emphasis, however, is not placed on what is provided, but on the impact and achieved outcomes. The Graduated Approach enables all practitioners and professionals to ask questions and revisit past decisions and provision.

### Practice questions

- Reflect on a child or young person's progress following an assessment period. Has the desired outcome been achieved? If not, why not? If yes, what was successful and why?
- Was the provision appropriate?
- Were the SMART targets effective (Specific, Measurable, Achievable, Relevant, Timed)?
- Was the assessment appropriate and accurate?

| Term 1 | Term 2 | Term 3 | Term 4 | | Term 5 | Term 6 |
|---|---|---|---|---|---|---|
| Assess | | Assess | | | Assess | Assess |

**Figure 4.2** Four times a year assessment model

### The Graduated Approach

This is a four-part cycle 'which draws on more detailed approaches, more frequent review and more specialist expertise in successive cycles in order to match interventions to the SEN of children and young people' (DfE and DoH, 2015: 6.44: 100). The Graduated Approach is to be used for children and young people requiring SEN support with or without an Education, Health and Care (EHC) plan. Although there are slight variations between early year provision, schools and colleges, the overall approach is the same. This four-part cycle is: Assess, Plan, Do and Review. If necessary, this cycle continues refining and becoming more specialist, if appropriate, on successive cycles. Different establishments carry out assessments at different times throughout an academic year. Some decide to assess at the end of the traditional seasonal terms (Autumn, Spring and Summer), while others assess six times a year on a short/half-term basis. However, some establishments are now assessing four times a year, recognising the benefits of accurate and recent data for the main academic transition time of the year, but also allowing enough work to be accomplished between assessment periods during the rest of the year. This would be managed in the way described in Figure 4.2.

#### *Assess*

*First cycle*: the class or subject teacher analyses the child's or young person's needs. This should draw on the following:

- the teacher's assessment and experience of the child or young person, e.g. class provision map, their progress and attainment;
- the progress review meetings, attendance figures, behaviour (detention or exclusion reports), peer comparison data;
- previous or other teacher assessments;
- national data (expected progress);
- views of parents/carers and the child and young person.

*Second cycle:* This will include all of the above once again, but might also include additional individualized assessments drilling down on the precise barriers to the child's or young person's learning. Helpful assessments for this might include:

- more in-depth assessments carried out by you or specialists within your establishment;
- observations carried out across a period of time;
- profiling tools;
- screening assessments, e.g. sensory needs or dyslexia.

*Third cycle:* Some progress may have been noted during the previous cycle of action, but, with parental agreement, external specialist assessments are considered

| | | |
|---|---|---|
| ACTION | ⟶ | Interventions, support, adjustments |
| EXPECTATIONS | ⟶ | Expected impact on progress and development |
| PROCESS | ⟶ | Who, what, when, how, by when |

**Figure 4.3** The AEP model

essential to provide further analysis of the child's or young person's needs. This might also include professionals from other disciplines. Following this, further cycles will follow, as long as the child or young person is identified as needing additional and different provision in order to progress and achieve their desired outcomes.

### *Plan*

At this point, the SEND Code of Practice states clearly that parents must be formally (in writing) informed that their child is going to be provided with SEN support. Of course I am sure this partnership working will have commenced (and should have) at the point of an initial concern.

Following the reflective and critical assessment process, the teacher, the SENCO, and the parents will agree at this point the AEP (Action, Expectations, Process) model (Figure 4.3).

**Practice question**

- Are whole school processes and systems in place to support the implementation and success of an AEP model?

### *Do*

This is where all the assessing and planning now needs to be implemented by the teacher. The class or subject teacher should remain responsible for the progress and development of all the children with SEN support, even if this involves them working with teaching assistants or specialist external or internal staff. As SENCO, your role is once again to ensure that the organization and recording of all input are consistent and universal across the establishment. However, you also will need to ensure that whatever was decided as part of the AEP design is workable in your environment. Do not agree to anything you cannot provide. Provide written minutes of these meetings and an individualized provision map which should be given to the parents as soon as possible, and also ensure that it is put in or on your record filing system so that professionals who need access to it can find it easily. Importantly, as mentioned earlier in the book, do not forget to set the review date at the first AEP meeting with the year included (e.g. 8.3.2016). NOTE: Ensure that you (or your SEN administrator) immediately book a room for the next meeting and that this agreed date fits in with your establishment's whole assessment and progress review time frame.

**Practice questions**

- Do we have the right staffing and expertise?
- Can the teacher or support staff or specialist plan and review together?
- Has this been costed and are the assessments evidence-based?
- Do further services need to be commissioned?
- Are further resources required?
- Is the physical environment/space available?

#### *Review*

Nursery staff, teachers and tutors are constantly reviewing and reflecting on their practice and on the progress of the children or young people they are working with. However, for the young people requiring additional and different SEN support, this process needs to be even more thorough, collaborative and on-going. As for all, the practitioners will be looking to ensure progress and targets for the children and young people with SEN have been achieved, but the sources of evidence might be much broader, including observations, questionnaires and additional and specialist assessments. As SENCO, you need to ensure that this work has taken place and that the additional assessments have been booked or commissioned in readiness for the next cycle of the Graduated Approach.

### Education, Health and Care (EHC) plans

The process of applying for an EHC plan will change for different phases, establishments and also geographical areas. Paperwork and consultation processes will now be developed locally. The SEND Code of Practice (DfE and DoH, 2015: 141–206) covers the assessment and plan process exceedingly thoroughly. It is therefore not my intention to replicate this information, but to provide you with an outline of what you need to consider prior to commencing the process.

Remember:

- An EHC assessment (like the former Statement assessment) will not always lead to an EHC plan.
- The statutory processes and timescales for an EHC assessment must be followed by local authorities and are fully detailed in the SEND Code of Practice (DfE and DoH, 2015: 154).
- The whole purpose of an EHC plan is 'to secure the best possible outcomes for them [child or young person] across education, health and social care and, as they get older, prepare them for adulthood' (DfE and DoH, 2015: 9.2: 142).
- The involvement of the child or young person and their family is vital.
- When agreeing outcomes, it is important to consider what is important *to* and *for* the child or young person.
- An EHC plan must not cease simply because a young person is aged 19 or over.
- An EHC plan must be formally reviewed at least annually, including those that are maintained after the young person has reached 19.

So what has changed? I expect if you are already a SENCO you can confidently tick off as recognizing the following as significant differences between the past Statements of Special Educational Needs and an Education, Health and Care plan.

An Education, Health and Care plan needs to be designed to do the following:

- to be accessible to parents, children and young people as well as practitioners;
- to focus on achieving outcomes;
- to co-ordinate provision across services where applicable;
- to be forward-looking – planning for significant transition points and for adult life.

Thus an EHC plan is not focused on what an educational establishment is providing, but on how they can remove the barriers to learning so that those with an EHC plan can achieve possible outcomes and also lead a fulfilled adult life as independently and productively as possible.

**Practice questions**

- Whether you are a nursery, school or college SENCO or SEN named person, do you analyse what the purpose of an EHC plan is and how it will benefit the child or young person?
- Do you set aside time to complete the EHC assessment based on the whole establishment identification of need? Is this written into your calendar (see Chapter 7) so that parental involvement, joint working and planning and assessment can be managed appropriately?
- Is your practice focused on outcomes, transitions and adulthood – even when you work in the early years? If not, why not? Your decisions may impact on the child's or young person's long-term outcomes and aspirations.

## 4.3 Provision management

As you can probably understand by now, a whole nursery, school or college approach to provision management is most effective to ensure that no child or young person fails to progress and achieve. By using this approach all children and young people can have their needs matched effectively to provision and outcomes. Also senior leaders, including the SENCO, can ensure all provision and approaches are value for money, evidence-based and thoroughly evaluated. Provision management, provision mapping and regular processes such as progress or department meetings can help you to strategically develop your whole school approach to additional and different support whether in the short or long term.

The processes and understanding explored in this section will help you to do the following:

- ensure decisions are informed by the insights of parents and those of children and young people themselves;
- have high ambitions and set stretching targets for them;
- track their progress towards these goals;
- keep under review the additional or different provision that is made for them;

- promote positive outcomes in the wider areas of personal and social development;
- ensure that the approaches used are based on the best possible evidence and are having the required impact on progress (DfE and DoH, 2015: 1.25: 25).

## Provision mapping systems

### *Class or individual provision maps*

There are many resources available to help you design your own establishment's provision mapping system, and one thing that is definite is that there is not one system that will be appropriate for all. It is understanding how you want to implement the system and for what purposes that is crucial in determining what your system looks like. Whatever you introduce needs to have the ability to work across the whole establishment and achieve a number of tasks. One word-based pro-forma, populated and managed by the class or subject teacher to track and evidence children's or young people's progress with additional intervention, is appropriate and is achievable within a relatively short period of time. These pro-formas may only need to include information such as:

- high quality teaching strategies and resources used within the group or class for all children or young people;
- start dates of targeted interventions and review dates (signed);
- the name of the intervention;
- how many children or young people are accessing this intervention, how frequently and with whom;
- pupil name, assessment level at entry point and again at the end point;
- outcome targets set. Don't forget, these targets need to be SMART (or even SMARTER – to include extending and rewarding).
- outcome target(s) achieved – none, partially, fully.

However, as SENCO, you need to construct, with the other leaders, a layered system which will also service many other elements of your tracking requirements.

### *Whole provision/school/college provision mapping*

These maps should be able to provide current and broad information not only for children or young people with SEN but for all the young people you are working with. These maps should indicate which interventions are provided for whom, by whom and the relevant timeframes. It is important, however, that you also have other really valuable information 'underneath'. If, for example, you use your intranet system or a specific software program which can generate planning and accounting information, you will be able to create different folders supporting the initial overall one. It is at this level that I believe a SENCO (and other leaders) should have information about:

- individual and class/group academic and social progress and achievement;
- the cost of resources;
- the cost of intervention;
- staff costs;
- research/marketing evidence of an intervention's or a strategy's effectiveness;

- information about the evidence of effectiveness of an intervention or a resource in relation to:
  (a) national data;
  (b) local data;
  (c) your establishment's data.

The whole establishment's mapping system should also be able to provide information about the academic progress for different vulnerable groups (e.g. pupil premium children and young people). In this way you can organize your provision management system to create the databases you require from which to analyse progress, the success (or not) of interventions and additional input, so that very early signs of lack of progress can quickly be identified and then appropriately supported.

### Progress/department meetings

As for the provision management system, progress/department meetings must be for all the children or young people in your establishment. It is no good just monitoring and critically reflecting on the progress and plans for children or young people already identified with having a special educational need or disability. As an inclusive educational provider, your establishment will want to ensure that a response to a child's lack of progress or sign of social or emotional distress, is recognized as soon as possible. Therefore, regular progress meetings which are committed dates in the provision/school or college diary, need to critically examine individual, group/class, whole establishment provision maps by the class teaching team, Senior Leaders and the SENCO. Local data, national data, expected targets and qualitative feedback can all be discussed at these meetings with particular focus on individual children and young people's progress, well-being and outcomes. These meetings will discuss those who are on the SEN register already, those who may need SEN support and those to whom you need to give short-term targeted support (academic or pastoral) and the overall progress of classes. Your role in these is to advocate at all times for the children, young people and families and to be able to voice your concerns about a particular intervention or strategy. As with anything, this system is only as robust as the people carrying them out and their expectations. This is why you need senior leaders:

- who will not allow these meetings to be suddenly cancelled (unless significant members of the team are indisposed);
- who will expect teachers to come to these meetings with their data updated on their provision maps and assessment sheets;
- who will expect teachers to have critically reflected on why some of their children or young people have not made progress and planned what they are going to do about it.

When progress meetings are embedded into practice at this level, you as SENCO will know that your colleagues are really recognizing and acknowledging that they have responsibility for the learning and well-being of all children or young people in their classrooms. Your role is to ensure they maintain the confidence, knowledge and skills to continue developing their professional expertise.

## 4.4 Transitions

During the past decade transitions have become seen as really important times for all children and young people, but especially for those with special educational needs. Many establishments and especially SENCOs now spend a great deal of their time ensuring that transitional arrangements are rigorous, active, visual both pre and post move. Moving between educational establishments and between year groups are nearly always considered carefully now with most using additional opportunities, summer camps/schools, individual passports and visual/colour and mentoring to aid children and young people to settle quickly with their needs being well prepared for.

However, when we look at recent statistics, it is clear that employment and successful independent living opportunities for people with special educational needs remain a national concern. Thus the SEND Code of Practice identifies transitions and life opportunities as a vital part of education provision and outcomes:

> Disabled people remain significantly less likely to be in employment than non-disabled people. In 2012, 46.3% of working-age disabled people are in employment compared to 76.4% of working-age non-disabled people. There is therefore a 30.1 percentage point gap between disabled and non-disabled people, representing over 2 million people.
>
> https://www.gov.uk/government/publications/disability-facts-and-figures/disability-facts-and-figures#employment (accessed 8 March 2016).

However, for specific areas of need, such as autism, employment rates drop dramatically with the National Autistic Society stating that: 'Only 16% of people with autism are in full time employment.' (http://www.autism.org.uk/007874) (accessed 16 March 2017).

A number of national charities and organizations help by providing advice online or give downloadable guidance materials (costs may apply) such as http://www.autism.org.uk/about/adult-life/work.aspx (accessed 8 March 2016).

Thus, this is another area where your role will be essential to help thinking, planning and preparing employers and work experience opportunities for young people with special educational needs. When I worked with nursery and Reception-aged children with special educational needs and their families, future independence and life opportunities were always on my mind.

**Practice questions**

- How do you help to prepare the children, young people and their families you work with for adulthood?
- Do you discuss issues with the future in mind?

Between Sections 7.37 and 8.8 of the SEND Code of Practice (DfE and DoH, 2015: 122–5) direction is provided for you to consider. It says that preparing for adulthood means preparing for:

- higher education or employment;
- independent living;
- participating in society;
- being healthy (7.38).

Whenever you work with children and young people, you know how important it is to focus on what they can do, their interests and motivations. This work needs to begin for children and young people with special educational needs in the early years and primary schools and not just be left for the secondary or college years.

**Case study 4.3 Preparation**

While working in a residential school, I noticed that preparation for living independently and work was frequently too little too late. Young people with special educational needs who were only 16 years old suddenly found themselves having to go and care for themselves with few independent living or employment skills. With support from employers and charities, a programme was developed by a careers specialist to help prepare the young people for life after they had left care. It was an intensive 24-hour programme for six weeks which focused on home DIY, budgeting, cooking, housework duties, CV writing, preparing for interviews and presentation. It was an amazing success with confident young people leaving the provision at the end of the academic year, knowing how to pay bills, open bank accounts and how to get through an interview and be offered employment.

Was this too little too late? Think about how you encourage employment and independent skills with the children or young people you work with. Could you and your establishment do more? Do you provide strategies, perhaps through Social Stories, for young people to practise in order to gain independence or skills to enable them to be confident within a business environment? This might be something as simple as using cutlery efficiently or smiling when they meet somebody. It is of course important to remember that at the end of the academic year in which they turn 16, young people with special educational needs, with or without an EHC plan, have the right to make requests and decisions themselves. How well is your school or college preparing them to manage this appropriately?

## 4.5 Mediation and the SEND Tribunal

The final section in this chapter reminds us that unfortunately at some time in your SENCO career you may find that parents or a young person disagree with the education service they are receiving. They then may wish to have access to the disagreement resolution service.

In other situations, parents and young people may seek mediation or even ask for a Tribunal. This is when your provision management organization, record keeping, minutes of meetings and conversations logged are vital, and why I have mentioned 'Don't forget to write the year.' Hopefully, however, your partnerships with parents and carers will be established through joint respect, good communication and openness, and thus such occurrences will be very rare.

Once again there are many details about each of these processes you will need to engage with, if this is a situation you find yourself in within the SEND Code of Practice, but the basic definitions are provided below.

### Disagreement resolution

These arrangements are 'designed to resolve disagreements about the performance of duties, SEN provision, disagreement over health and social care provision and disagreements between health commissioners and local authorities and are voluntary for both parties' (DfE and DoH, 2015; 11.13: 251).

#### *Mediation*

Mediation is linked specifically to decisions about EHC assessments and EHC plans.

#### *Tribunal*

A Tribunal hears:

- disability discrimination claims against schools and against a local authority where it is the responsible body for a school;
- appeals against decisions made by local authorities in England in relation to EHC assessments and EHC plans (DfE and DoH, 2015: 11.42: 259).

## What does this mean for the SENCO?

*The following are a few questions or suggestions which will hopefully aid you in either establishing an effective provision management system or enhancing specific areas of your work still further.*

- *Do all your staff understand the Graduated Approach and their role within this? If not, how are you going to solve either the lack of knowledge and understanding, or their willingness to accept their responsibilities? Can you use performance management methods if required (as the last resort of course)?*
- *Gain the support of all the senior leadership team before introducing and preparing staff for a move from Individual Education Plans (IEP) to provision mapping for all children or young people, including those with SEN.*
- *Carefully consider who and how such a change is going to be implemented. What type of support/external input is going to be required?*
- *Carry out an audit of resources available in all classrooms and note which ones are used well and consistently?*

- *Then write a list of the resources and equipment needed to ensure that universal strategies and resources can help minor or intermittent support for all children or young people.*
- *Within your strategic plan, review equipment, including furniture and lighting equipment, with your three-year SEN strategic and accessibility plans in mind.*
- *Review all of your pro-formas, checklists, letters and recording systems to ensure that they all link appropriately and are accessible to parents and children or young people.*
- *Evaluate the level of SEN administration and support you receive. Also review contracts for all the adults working with children or young people specifically with SEN.*
- *Review the assessments you have available, what they are for and who can carry them out.*
- *Reflect on where you require external specialist support and ensure that the specialists all provide you with what you need (i.e. value for money).*

## Direct links to the SEND Code of Practice

- vi It includes guidance on the joint planning and commissioning of services to ensure close co-operation between education, health and social care.
- 1.24 Special educational provision is underpinned by high quality teaching and is compromised by anything less.
- 2.21 Local authorities should adopt a key working approach, which provides children, young people and parents with a single point of contact to help ensure the holistic provision and co-ordination of services and support.
- 5.26 The EYFS profile provides parents, practitioners and teachers with a well-rounded picture of a child's knowledge, understanding and abilities.
- 5.36 It is particularly important in the early years that there is no delay in making any necessary special educational provision.
- 6.4 School leaders and teaching staff, including the SENCO, should identify any patterns in the identification of SEN, both within the school and in comparison with national data, and use these to reflect on and reinforce the quality of teaching.
- 6.5 The identification of SEN should be built into the overall approach to monitoring the progress and development of all pupils.
- 6.18 It can include progress in areas other than attainment – for instance, where a pupil needs to make additional progress with wider development or social needs in order to make a successful transition to adult life.
- 6.19 The first response to such progress should be high quality teaching targeted at their areas of weakness. Where progress continues to be less than expected, the class or subject teacher, working with the SENCO, should assess whether the child has SEN.
- 6.57 SEN support should include planning and preparation for the transitions between phases of education and preparation for adult life.
- 6.76 Provision maps are an efficient way of showing all the provision that the school makes which is additional to and different from that which is offered

through the school's curriculum. The use of provision maps can help SENCOs to maintain an overview of the programmes and interventions used with different groups of pupils and provide a basis for monitoring the levels of intervention.

- 6.77 Provision management can be used strategically to develop special educational provision to match the assessed needs of pupils across the school, and to evaluate the impact of that provision on pupil progress. Used in this way, provision management can also contribute to school improvement by identifying particular patterns of need and potential areas of development for teaching staff. It can help the school to develop the use of interventions that are effective and to remove those that are less so. *It can support schools to improve their core offer for all pupils as the most effective approaches are adopted more widely across the school.*
- 7.23 Where, despite the college having taken relevant and purposeful action to identify, assess and meet the needs of the student, the student is still not making the expected progress, the college or young person should consider requesting an EHC needs assessment.
- 7.29 Like mainstream schools, colleges are expected to provide appropriate, high quality SEN support using all available resources.

## Resources

This resource is available to help young people with autism prepare for employment: http://www.autism.org.uk/about/adult-life/work.aspx (accessed 8 March 2016).

# 5 The personalized learning environment

**Introduction**

For the purposes of this chapter the 'learning environment' refers to a school, nursery, specialist provision or any other educational establishment. The importance of the learning environment for all children and young people and especially those with special educational needs is frequently underestimated. How well do you integrate and actively demonstrate theories of learning in practice and policy? Our own physical surroundings can also impact significantly on how we as adults feel, perform and engage with learning. For example, if you have to sit in a cold conference room on the floor, your ability to concentrate and engage, let alone control your temper, will, I suspect, be seriously affected. How often though do we as teachers and SENCOs think about the physical and sensory needs of our pupils? How suitable are our environments for all pupils and how do we ensure we consider these factors when designing new buildings, purchase new furniture or equipment and plan lessons or interventions? This chapter will therefore help you to expand your understanding and knowledge of how to create or develop your establishment into an inclusive environment where theory and practice support and reinforce decisions. Each learning environment is unique, but there are clear actions you can take which will provide you with ideas and solutions to potential barriers to learning and teaching for children and young people (and adults) wherever you work.

## 5.1 Theories of learning

### Childhood and learning

Childhood is a relatively modern concept (Zelizer, 1994) with definitions varying between countries and cultures. Generally, it can be said that western countries now see childhood as a time of innocence when children play and are educated and are financially and economically provided for. However, this is not the case globally and even though the United Nations Convention on the Rights of the Child (1989) was ratified by 194 member states, with Article 13 saying that all children have the right to freedom of expression, children's rights are not accepted or upheld universally. With a growing multi-cultural society in the UK, it is therefore immensely important that SENCOs and all educators remember that children arriving in the UK or travelling between areas will have diverse life experiences determined by their own cultural background and circumstances. Thus, as Prout (2005) says, we cannot assume that all families, communities and children see childhood in the same way and therefore our learning environments need to acknowledge this as a factor when considering our teaching, interventions or provision.

Although the designation of your education establishment will need specific actions, you will need to think about the cultural needs and experiences of the children in terms of the learning environment. Use the list in Box 5.1 to help you consider how effective your establishment is in understanding how some members of your community might view childhood from a different cultural or experiential background.

**Box 5.1 Factors to consider when exploring differing views of childhood and education**

- *The adult role*: politeness, gender, eye contact, asking questions.
- *Gender*: seating position, social opportunities, play.
- *Play:* acceptable for which age/gender group and type of play.
- *Social expectations*: clothing, hair styles, social relationships.
- *Employment*: when would they be expected to earn for the family?
- *Family position*: status and position within a family may be important.
- *Academic expectations*: recognition and desires of children versus family expectations.
- *Disability*: visible or invisible/acceptance or denial.
- *Special educational needs*: potential for all/opportunities for all.
- *Privacy*: involvement of agencies or staff.
- *Language*: spoken and gesture (non-verbal).
- *Food and drink*: how, what and when (in private or in a social situation).
- *Religious understanding and requirements*: opportunities to practise and share.
- *Dress, hair and make-up*: cultural, religious or family preference.

As you can see, this list is not only useful for early years settings, but for all ages and all designations. From this you can begin to enhance and develop your practices trying to recognize how your own establishment's beliefs and values might impact on learning, especially for children and young people with special educational needs or disabilities.

At this juncture it is important to critically reflect on your own views about learning. After reading the Reflection below, consider what you believe and how this might or definitely does impact on your work as a SENCO. Would all teachers and educators in your establishment believe the same? How might differing views impact on practice? Would it influence how and what provision is put in place and for whom?

**Reflection**

*Do you believe that every child begins to learn within the womb and that learning continues throughout life? My own view is that learning is extremely complex, and that while some learning is incidental and creative, other learning is directed and purposeful. I passionately believe in Bronfenbrenner's ecological model of child development and that the environment (community and social world) is influenced by and influences a child. In our ever-changing world I feel that this is the case now more than ever before. I have experienced children's learning influenced by the media and their culture (Bronfenbrenner), as well as their physical, emotional and motivational state (Maslow). I think that knowledge is gained through experiences, and that learning is interactive and should be enjoyable (Locke). Like Rousseau, I believe that education should be able to follow a child's natural interests and be child-centred (Dewey, Montessori, Froebel), while also recognizing that the economic and social needs of society have to be met.*

### Learning and theory

Both 'learning' and 'theory' need to be defined. Very simply, *learning* can be defined as the acquisition of skill or knowledge (David et al., 2011) and a *theory* as a set of principles or statements which can be used to 'explain a group of facts or phenomena' (Gray and MacBlain, 2012: 3). I expect you have memories of learning about a number of learning theories in college or university and you will have your favourites which influence your teaching approach to this day. How good are you at demonstrating through your leadership role, a dynamic relationship between practice and theory in everyday practice?

Without doubt there have been many influential philosophical and empirical theories of learning over the centuries which have attempted to both explain and define aspects of human learning. Some of the most significant theories of learning, together with their strengths and weaknesses, have been included in Table 5.1 for you as a quick reference sheet.

### Practice suggestions

- Use Table 5.1 to help you determine which theory or theories of learning influence your establishment's development.
- Audit staff to see if your findings concur with their views. Determine how your collective preferred theories of learning need to be reflected in your curriculum, interventions and policies such as SEN and behaviour.

### Practice questions

- Are you aware of which learning theories influence your own and your colleagues practice?
- How do you incorporate learning theories into your policies, curriculum and ethos?

**Table 5.1** Some aspects of key learning theories

| *Aspects of learning theories* | *Founding fathers* | | | | *Classical respondent conditioning* | *Operant conditioning* | *Cognitive constructivism* | *Social constructivism* | *Ecological systems model* | *Discovery learning* | *New social studies of childhood* |
|---|---|---|---|---|---|---|---|---|---|---|---|
| | *LOCKE* | *DEWEY* | *MONTES-SORI* | *STEINER* | *PAVLOV* | *SKINNER* | *PIAGET* | *VYGOTSKY* | *BRONFEN-BRENNER* | | *NSSC* |
| Knowledge and understanding of the world through 'sensory experience.' | √ | √ | √ | √ | | | √ | √ | √ | | |
| Important to learn how to learn | √ | | √ | √ | | | | | | | |
| Learning should be enjoyable; importance of creative play | √ | | | | | | √ | √ | √ | √ | √ |
| Important for young children to learn | √ | | √ | √ | | | | | | | |
| Child-centred education – under-standing children's experiences | | √ | √ | √ | | | √ | √ | | | √ |
| Children need support and direction by an adult to understand the world | | √ | √ | | | | | √ | | | |
| Each individual child is unique | | √ | √ | √ | | | | | √ | | |
| Education and society linked; culture | | √ | | √ | | | | √ | √ | | √ |
| Interests of children to be treated as important | | √ | | | | | | √ | | | |
| Schools to be viewed as an extension of the home and wider community | | √ | | | | | | √ | √ | √ | |

*(Continued)*

**Table 5.1** (continued)

| | | | | | | | | | | | |
|---|---|---|---|---|---|---|---|---|---|---|---|
| Emphasis placed on the learning environment | | | √ | √ | | | √ | √ | | | |
| Virtue and courtesy | √ | √ | √ | √ | | | | | | | |
| Education needs to respond to the changing physical, cognitive, social and emotional needs of children | | | | √ | | | √ | √ | √ | | |
| Children are passive in the learning process | | | | | √ | | | | | | |
| See child development in terms of stages | | | | | | | √ | | | | |
| Learning is based on associations – ‘stimulus–response’. | | | | | √ | √ | | | | | |
| Children are active participants in the learning process – learning is voluntary | √ | √ | √ | √ | | √ | √ | √ | √ | √ | √ |
| Learning is based on association between behaviour and its consequences | | | | | | √ | | | | | |
| Focuses on the importance of a child’s readiness to learn | | | | | | | √ | | | | |
| Children born with basic cognitive skills | | | | | | | √ | √ | | | |
| Importance of language in mediat-ing thinking and learning | √ | | | | | | | √ | | √ | |
| Zone of Proximal Development (ZPD) | | | | | | | | √ | | | |
| Peer collaboration | | | | | | | √ | √ | √ | √ | √ |
| Important to develop a child’s potential | | | | | | | √ | √ | √ | √ | √ |

One significant point you will note from Table 5.1 is that while each theoretical perspective has strengths and weaknesses, none of them can completely explain how children learn. Thus you may draw on several learning theories to help you develop your practice rather than remain aligned to a single theory.

Perhaps not surprisingly, this lack of a complete explanation of children's learning has led in in recent years to a new disciplinary approach emerging. This newly evolving theoretical framework is called the 'new social studies of childhood' (NSSC) or the new sociology of childhood. Gray and MacBlain (2012: 124) consider this term to be an approach which positions 'the child at the heart of the discussion'. The NSSC seeks to hear the voice of the child, to be multidisciplinary in its approach and to recognize children as individuals who have rights in line with the United Nations Convention on the Rights of the Child (UNCRC) principles. Although still a very new paradigm with acknowledged weaknesses, you can see that the NSSC theoretical framework is reflected in some current national (English) documentation and legislation, particularly with regard to children and young people with special educational needs.

## 5.2 A personalized environment

An educational establishment, whether for 3-year-olds or 19-year-olds, needs to ensure that a whole school approach to providing an effective and energising environment is actively promoted for all. Thought about broadly, the 'learning environment' encompasses all aspects of a child or young person's situation. As a SENCO, you need to think about this for the children and young people you are specifically focused on enabling, as when viewed in isolation, aspects of the environment can unfortunately have more influence than they should on a child's or young person's educational experience and thus on outcomes (educational, social and emotional). It is important to consider at all times what a child or young person with a special educational need is experiencing and what impacts on this. The physical environment and safety and well-being will be discussed separately in greater detail in Sections 5.3 and 5.4.

Figures 5.1 and 5.2 illustrate the complexity of a learning environment for a child or young person and especially those with a special educational need. The

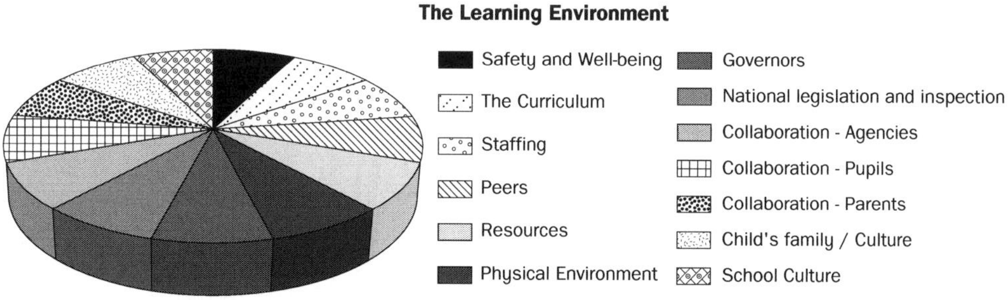


**Figure 5.1** A well-balanced learning environment where many significant factors for children with a SEN are managed in a whole school approach

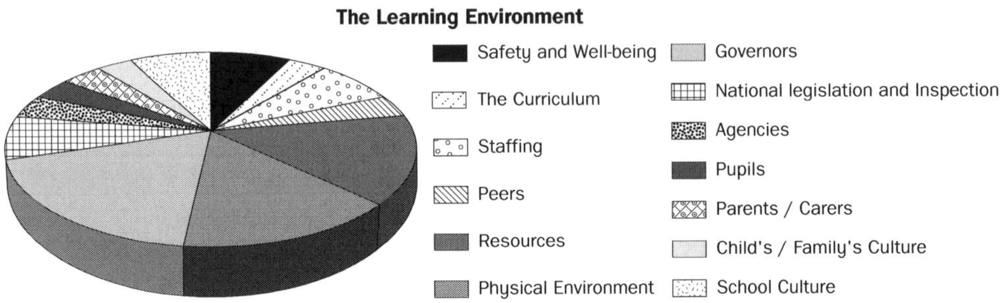


**Figure 5.2** Factors which are negatively impacting on the learning environment of a school

percentage size of each suggested section in Figure 5.1 will vary for your establishment, depending on your specific situation, and these headings are by no means exclusive. Using the headings supplied in Figure 5.1 or your own, create your establishment's pie chart, identifying by the size of each section which factors are felt to be currently, either positively or negatively, impacting on the learning environment of the children or young people with a SEN. A simple questionnaire can be written focusing on asking specific questions about each of these areas. Using closed questions and a Likert scale can help you analyse your findings and construct a similar pie chart to Figure 5.1. To be most effective, this questionnaire needs to be completed by as many stakeholders as possible, but particularly the staff, governors, parents/carers of children with a SEN and the children (if appropriate) with a SEN.

Figure 5.1 demonstrates a learning environment in which all contributing factors work in an integrated manner in recognition of the needs of all children and young people. However, Figure 5.2 provides a visual representation for the SENCO to use of the factors which could be impacting negatively on the effectiveness of the learning environment for children with a SEN. Here you can see that resourcing, the physical environment and the Governor role are not providing the most positive contributions possible. You can perhaps also see that these factors are beginning to influence the culture of the school and the safety and well-being of the children, some of whom will have a special educational need. All of this information can then be used to help develop practice and training, and encourage allocation of funding.

It is also recognized that this is one area of your work as a SENCO that will have clear practical differences depending on the age group you are working with. To help you think about this for your own situation, Table 5.2 has been constructed as an exemplar using the four areas of need as defined in the SEND Code of Practice (DfE and DoH, 2015). Can you see on completion of your charts and table how important understanding your theoretical framework is in relation to creating a really inclusive learning environment?

## 5.3 The physical and sensory environment

Both the physical and sensory environment are extremely important for any child or young person with a special educational need. If we do not take full

**Table 5.2** Factors which can impact on the learning environment for pupils with different types of special educational needs

| *Areas of need* | *Communication and interaction* | *Cognition and learning* | *Social, emotional and mental health difficulties* | *Sensory and/or physical needs* |
|---|---|---|---|---|
| Safety and well-being | Lack of visual resources to support pupils' understanding | | | |
| The curriculum | Pupils are not provided with interventions, e.g. speech and language therapy | | | |
| Staffing | Staff do not have awareness training | | | |
| Peers | Peers will interpret pupils' needs to adults | | | |
| Resources | No visual symbols or Makaton available | | | |
| Physical environment | Large rooms with wooden floor, no blinds on windows | | | |
| Governors | Little understanding of the needs for specialist teachers and resources | | | |
| National legislation and inspection | This is not fully understood by all teachers. No training provided. | | | |
| Collaboration – agencies | Can access only limited NHS speech and language therapy for pupils with severe needs | | | |
| Collaboration – parents | Parents find it hard to attend clinics | | | |
| Collaboration – pupils | Pupils are frequently taught separately with others with similar needs | | | |
| Child's or family's culture | This area of need can be difficult for families from some cultures to understand. Difficulties can be concealed because English is an additional language | | | |
| School culture | Pupils with SEN/D are still removed from class for interventions | | | |

consideration of these issues. they can truly impact on their self-esteem, well-being and life opportunities. We all have different sensory and environmental preferences, but the majority of us are able to adapt or alter our situations to suit our needs. Frequently children are unable to determine their situations in an educational environment, because they are told where to sit, where to go and

*Observer: Pupil/Teacher/Support Staff/Parent/Governor/SENCO (circle one)*

*Date:_________________*

*Part of School/Setting/College:________________________*

| *Senses* | *Communication and interaction* | *Cognition and learning* | *Social, emotional and mental health difficulties* | *Sensory and/or physical needs* |
|---|---|---|---|---|
| **Taste**<br>Location:<br>Issue:<br>P/S:<br>Changes: | | | | |
| **Hearing**<br>Location:<br>Issue:<br>P/S:<br>Changes: | | | | |
| **Smell**<br>Location:<br>Issue:<br>P/S:<br>Changes: | | | | |
| **Sight**<br>Location:<br>Issue:<br>P/S:<br>Changes: | | | | |
| **Touch**<br>Location:<br>Issue:<br>P/S:<br>Changes: | | | | |
| **Proprioception**<br>Location:<br>Issue:<br>P/S:<br>Changes: | | | | |
| **Vestibular**<br>Location:<br>Issue:<br>P/S:<br>Changes: | | | | |

**Key:** P = Pupil
S = Staff

**Figure 5.3** An audit checklist of the sensory environment using the SEN broad areas of need

*Observer: Pupil/Teacher/Support Staff/Parent/Governor/SENCO (circle one)*

*Date:_________________*

*Part of School/Setting/College:________________________*

| *Places:* | *Communication and interaction* | *Cognition and learning* | *Social, emotional and mental health difficulties* | *Sensory and/or physical needs* |
|---|---|---|---|---|
| **Hall**<br>Issue:<br>P/S:<br>Changes: | | | | |
| **Reception area:**<br>Issue:<br>P/S:<br>Changes: | | | | |
| **Restaurant**<br>Issue:<br>P/S:<br>Changes: | | | | |
| **Head teacher's office**<br>Issue:<br>P/S:<br>Changes: | | | | |
| **Toilets (location)**<br>Issue:<br>P/S:<br>Changes: | | | | |
| **Changing rooms (N/A)**<br>Issue:<br>P/S:<br>Changes: | | | | |
| **Classroom 1**<br>Issue:<br>P/S:<br>Changes: | | | | |

**Key:** P = Pupil
S = Staff

**Figure 5.4** An audit checklist of the physical environment using the SEN broad areas of need

Source: DfE and DoH (2015).

what to do. Most children will develop strategies and skills to help them manage these incidences, but those with a special educational need may experience these as barriers and be unable to adapt and engage when they are physically or sensory uncomfortable. To ensure that you are not missing these factors for your pupils, it is sensible to carry out whole school setting audits, including room plans with furniture, lighting and other equipment *in situ*. If possible (time and availability) form a working party which can include some of your pupils with physical or sensory needs, parents, and teachers, to undertake both a physical and sensory audit of your educational environment. Each situation will be different depending on the building, the locality and the needs of the children and young people and staff. Some of the changes required will need to be ameliorated immediately because of the needs of your current children, while others can be considered within your three- or five-year plans. Wherever possible, seek support and direction from a paediatric occupational therapist who will be able to help you identify significant factors for children with a special educational need.

Start this audit work with charts which could look like the ones found in Figures 5.3 and 5.4. The simpler the better, because it allows the observer the flexibility to include what they feel could be an issue for children with a specific need. A parent/carer or child might have already indicated that there could be an issue with, for example, body odour or artificial lighting, and the audit could provide evidence to support their views. However, there are already many observational sheets already available; some are focused on children with special needs such as autism (Autism Education Trust and the National Strategies Inclusion Development Programme materials). Such audits will indicate general issues and concerns, but as a SENCO you will also need to be able to identify specific issues for individual children.

### Case study 5.1 The trouble with furniture and . . . .

A nursery and primary school share the same location for lunch times. The lunch hall has tables and seats which are fixed together and are of the same height for all the children, plastic meal trays and adult-sized cutlery. The lunch hall is not large enough for everyone to eat together and so a rota system is necessary. The lunchtime staff support the children as well as they can, but the children are often required to move out into the playground as soon as is possible. There is one member of senior management on duty in the lunch hall.

Issues resulting from this situation:

- The lunch hall is very noisy.
- Many packed lunches/school lunches are not all eaten.
- There is a lot of mess left on the floor and tables in the hall.
- There are many behavioural issues reported during and immediately after lunch times.

### Practice questions

- Why are lunch times such as problem?
- Can the children sit comfortably at the lunch tables?
- Can their feet touch the ground and why is this important?
- Are the size of the cutlery and the trays appropriate?

- Who is modelling good eating skills (e.g. chewing, cutting), turn taking when speaking and good posture for digestion?
- If young children are told off for falling from a seat or bench, what could be causing this?

**Practice suggestions**

- Take time on a couple of days to observe the children move around and eat in the lunch hall. What do you notice happens? What do they find difficult to do? Is the seating suitable and are the tables at the correct height?
- See if it is possible to buy a few pieces of cutlery which is a suitable size for younger children and practise their use in class with play dough, for example. This can also be carried out with eating implements the children from other cultures will wish to use.
- At morning breaks if you provide fruit, emphasize the importance of chewing well and remind children to chew all of their lunch well. This is so important for speech development.
- If at all possible, encourage staff or older pupils to sit with the children to act as a role model or table monitor and make the lunch time an important learning session.

### Secondary-aged young people

The SENCO in a secondary school might ask, what do these factors matter to the young people I work with? The answer is a lot. If appropriate cutlery skills, chewing skills, posture, turn-taking and social skills are not in place by the time they arrive in a secondary environment, the greater freedom encouraged around lunch time can impact significantly on young people.

Think about these questions and suggested answers:

- *What foods will young people select if they cannot use eating utensils?*
- Answer: finger foods, e.g. pizza, chips, pasties, cake.
- Outcomes: poor diet and possible obesity and long-term discomfort if asked to go for a business lunch. Also these skills support hand/eye control and manipulative skills.
- *How could poor chewing skills and poor posture impact on young people?*
- Answer: poor speech production which could then also impact on reading, writing and self-confidence; poor digestion.
- *How can conversation skills and turn-taking assist young people?*
- Answer: In a business/work environment young people will have many everyday opportunities to practise listening, developing a conversation and speaking in turn.

As a 'vital lesson for all', lunch times can provide valuable lessons for many aspects of a child's and young person's development – not just nutrition – and a cleaner and quieter hall. It can also give children with motor, speech or social needs additional positive opportunities to practise their skills and therefore lessen the need for individual SEN intervention.

And of course the lunch hall is not the only place in an educational environment where colour, furniture, lighting and equipment can be considered when looking at how barriers can be removed for children at a whole school or class level.

Not all needs will be met with this whole school approach and if this is the case, the next step is to carry out observations of individual children who are causing on-going concern and where it is felt a sensory perceptual need could be part of the issue. Figure 5.5 is a simple observation chart all staff will be able to use appropriately. If there are concerns, this will highlight them, especially if several observations take place both in the same location and in other areas of the building or establishment.

When all of these pieces of evidence are collected together, you will be able to consider which are urgent changes to practise, location, furniture or equipment to meet the needs of children with special educational needs. Repeat these activities at least annually.

### *Action*

1 Audit of physical environment, including furniture and equipment (working party).
2 Audit of sensory environment (working party).
3 Room plans generated.
4 Observations.
5 Discussions with parents/pupils/staff.

| Spend 10 minutes observing a child with a possible physical or sensory perceptual need. What factors can you see that may be causing this child a problem? What can you or the teacher do about it? How can you change the environment to solve these issues? | | | | | | | |
|---|---|---|---|---|---|---|---|
| What does the pupil appear to see/have problems seeing? | What does the pupil appear to hear/not hear? | Who and what touches the pupil? | What/how does the child touch? | What does the pupil appear to smell: positive/negative? | What forms of communication does he/she appear to understand/not understand? (think about distances here as well) | General observations | Minutes |
| | | | | | | | |

**Figure 5.5** Observation chart

Finally, do not forget to talk to and consider the needs of staff as well. I have known teachers who have had to leave their posts because of the environment, e.g. too noisy, too hot or too much glass.

## 5.4 A safe environment

Education settings are generally very safe places today for children and young people with rigorous processes and regulations in place. Staff are all screened (Disclosure and Barring Service (DBS) checks) prior to commencing a new post (and hopefully every three years at least afterwards) and visitors are welcomed, but have to be accompanied or show a DBS certificate if working with children without a member of staff present. Safeguarding procedures must be in place and trained staff have designated roles to ensure all young people are given the support they require and a safe and secure environment in which to learn. However, for children and young people with a special educational need, providing a safe environment can be much more complex and it is important that the SENCO is always involved in updating policies and any training or input provided for pupils. If as SENCO you are not a designated safeguarding officer or involved in the writing of risk assessments for trips or additional activities, or for policies such as bullying and behaviour, then you need to ask to be included in consultations. This is vital to ensure that consideration is given to how policies and procedures are experienced by all children and young people.

This can once again be managed using a tiered approach. At a whole establishment level, for example, the behaviour or bullying policies need to consider how a child with a SEN like autism might experience them. Do they include appendices or different outcomes dependent on factors, such as communication needs or autism? This is important, I suggest, so that there is transparency about how matters will be managed for staff, parents/carers and pupils. Another example of how an educational establishment can show it is thinking inclusively is to ensure it has many visual supports in place throughout the whole site to enable children with language, communication and hearing needs to get around independently.

The next tier would involve the SENCO in getting in specialist support from a speech and language therapist or occupational therapist, for example, to ensure that training and activities involving a whole year group are appropriate and meaningful for children with specific needs. A good example of this is sex education for young people with a communication need, or for primary-aged children with autism or ADHD about keeping safe.

An additional session or personalized resources should support these events and activities and the SENCO needs to ensure they are in place.

Staff also need to be provided with training by the SENCO (or organized by the SENCO) to ensure that they know what to look out for when working with children with specific additional needs and disabilities. This is particularly true around safeguarding and how to recognize signs of abuse in children with a disability such as autism. There are resources to help you (see section on Resources), but this type of training needs to be whole establishment and repeated as regularly as possible and for all age groups.

The final tier needs to be led by the SENCO and teachers, and is when an individualized plan is needed for a child to ensure they have a safe environment in which to learn. Using tools as illustrated above and especially observations, discussions with parents and other professionals can help identify and therefore correctly target required changes to the environment to enable a child to remain calm, engaged and comfortable. Can you imagine what it is like when you don't know where you are in a building or where you have to go to ask for help or advice, especially if on a trip or school holiday? A slight adjustment in a policy, training scheme or activity can help keep children and young people with a special educational need safe and help them become independent, but how often do you think about asking this type of question or adapt and personalize specialist input or activity?

Thus, the physical and sensory learning environment needs to be as inclusive as it can be generically with attention paid, using a tiered approach, as described above, to issues which some children will find difficult to manage because of their individual needs. Only then can the most beneficial changes or interventions be made. Don't forget it might be something very simple such as changing the colour of a book, putting in a blind or writing a social story, but you will not know this unless observations of the child or children, and discussions with other stakeholders are carried out.

## What does this mean for the SENCO?

- *It is important that a SENCO recognizes and engages with the theories of learning that influence the teachers' practice.*
- *The SENCO also needs to understand the impact the environment might be having on all learners, but especially on children and young people with a special educational needs and/or a disability.*
- *The SENCO needs to recognize the importance of their involvement in determining policy.*
- *The SENCO also needs to ensure that training and materials on important matters such as safe care, sexual health and personal care are appropriate and accessible for pupils with special educational needs.*
- *The SENCO also need to ensure suitable training is given to all teachers about how to recognize when a child or young person with a special need might present if they are experiencing abuse or neglect.*

## Direct links to the SEND Code of Practice

- xx Schools and local authority. . . must publish accessibility plans setting out how they plan to increase access for disabled pupils to the curriculum, the physical environment and to information.
- xxii Where a child or young person is covered by SEN and disability legislation, reasonable adjustments and access arrangements should be considered as part of SEN planning and review.
- 1.2 Principles underpinning the Code of Practice include:
  - a focus on inclusive practice and removing barriers to learning;
  - successful preparation for adulthood, including independent living and employment.

- 6.3 School leaders should regularly review how expertise and resources used to address SEN can be used to build the quality of whole school provision as part of their approach to school improvement.
- 6.62 The SENCO and class teacher, together with the specialists, and involving the pupil's parents, should consider a range of evidence-based and effective teaching approaches, appropriate equipment, strategies and interventions in order to support the child's progress. They should agree the outcomes to be achieved through the support, including a date by which progress will be reviewed.
- 6.97 The SENCO, headteacher and governing body or proprietor should establish a clear picture of the resources that are available to the school. They should consider their strategic approach to meeting SEN in the context of the total resources.
- 7.22 The governing bodies of colleges should ensure that all staff interact appropriately and inclusively with students who have SEN or a disability and should ensure they have appropriate expertise within their workforce.

## Resources

1 The College of Occupational Therapist information sheet clearly details the key facts and information about the roles and responsibilities of Occupational Therapists. It states:

> Occupational therapy is a person-centred profession concerned with promoting a balanced range of occupations to enhance health and wellbeing. Occupations refer to everything people do in the course of their daily life . . . Children and young people may experience disruption to their occupations due to injury, illness or disability, family circumstances, or at times of transition . . . Occupational therapists will spend time finding out about the child . . . and what they want, need or are expected to do. They will then work together with the child, family and other key people to evaluate what helps or hinders their involvement in daily life roles. Together, possible solutions will be developed, such as exploring alternative ways of doing things or making changes to the environment to support participation.
>
> https://www.cot.co.uk/sites/default/files/general/public/Children-and-Young-People-updated-April2015.pdf (accessed 17 January 2016).

2 The Autism Education Trust offers a free resource which can be downloaded and which provides guidance about what professionals need to consider with regards to safeguarding and child protection for children and young people with autism. http://www.autismeducationtrust.org.uk/resources/safeguarding.aspx (accessed 17 January 2016).

3 The Disclosure and Barring Service Check (previously CRB) offers a very useful direct link. It is important that these are carried out for *all* staff and I would suggest at least every three years: https://www.gov.uk/disclosure-barring-service-check/overview (accessed 30. January 2016). Only employers and licensing bodies can request a DBS and there is a useful guidance for

employers' page on the website as well: https://www.gov.uk/guidance/dbs-check-requests-guidance-for-employers (accessed 7 March 2016).

4 The government website provides you with very helpful information about sharing advice for safeguarding purposes. This latest guidance document published in March 2015 and updated in September 2016, called *Keeping Children Safe in Education,* will help you decide when and with whom you share personal information: https://www.gov.uk/government/publications/safeguarding-practitioners-information-sharing-advice (accessed 2 October 2016).

# 6 Working together

This is another key part of any SENCO's work and needs to be a crucial element of what makes an educational establishment outstanding. As a SENCO, you will need the interpersonal and communication skills to work alongside and with a whole range of different stakeholders. Some of these stakeholders will work with statutory agencies while others may work for businesses, or with councils or the government. Then, of course, there will be the voluntary and charitable sector workers, including governors or trustees. However, without doubt, the children and young people with a special educational need and disability themselves, and their families and carers are the most important people. Unfortunately, our professional frameworks and working practices, and especially our time limitations frequently encourage us to pay 'lip-service' to working in a truly child- or young person-centric manner.

## 6.1 Children and young people as partners

> Children, who are capable of forming views, have a right to receive and make known information, to express an opinion, and to have that opinion taken into account in any matters affecting them. The views of the child should be given due weight according to the age, maturity and capability of the child.
>
> (UNICEF, 1989: Articles 12 and 13)

I do not expect any of you would disagree with the point of view that for a SENCO the outcomes of children or young people with special educational needs and disabilities are key to how well you are seen to fulfil your role by your colleagues, managers and even Ofsted. I think that all SENCOs would also say that it is vital to identify any learning need (whether it is considered a SEN or not) for any child or young person as early as possible in order to begin to achieve this for all. As discussed earlier, on-going tracking and rigorous assessment regimes are the main tool that educational establishments will use to regularly monitor progress and achievement. This provides very clear quantitative data, and I would agree progress review meetings will also provide the professional qualitative reasons and views for lack of progress or excellent achievement. Note, however, that it is much harder to sustain on-going participation and engagement with children and young people about their progress and provision.

The increasing priority given to hearing the voices of children or young people with special educational needs has increased during the past three decades, with Articles 12 and 13 (UNICEF, 1989) being the most significant international agreement focused on this aspect of children's rights. This meant that in 1994 the positive impact of the involvement of the child was recognized. The original Code of Practice (DfE, 1994: 2:34–2:36, 14–15) said, 'The effectiveness of any assessment and intervention will be influenced by the involvement and interest of the child or young person concerned' and there was great emphasis placed on their involvement and views. However, the language used was weak, saying that schools should consider how, for example they 'involve pupils in decision-making processes' (DfE, 1994: 2:37, 15). In many ways this approach did not encourage educational settings to really focus on robustly enhancing their practice in this area and SENCOs, because of lack of whole school commitment, would often end up just showing children and young people what had been decided for their Individual Education Plans (IEP) and asking for their agreement. And what child would say 'no'?

The revised SEN Code of Practice (DfES, 2001a: 27) and the SEN Toolkit (DfES, 2001c) had a chapter on pupil participation, highlighting the right of children and young people 'with special educational needs to be involved in making decisions and exercising choices'. Here the views and unique knowledge of their own special educational needs were identified as reasons for the children and young people themselves to participate in decision-making about their own provision, reviews and outcomes. But, despite saying that the 'principle of seeking and taking account of the ascertainable views of the child or young person is an important one' (DfES, 2001a: 3:3, 27), it also warned about 'overburdening' them. Once again, however, this appropriate caution seemingly gave a reason not to take this work forward more rigorously in schools and thus led to only slow and arguably insignificant change in practice regarding hearing and responding to the voice of the child. This was until the findings of the Lamb Inquiry (DCSF, 2009a) were published. This Inquiry looked at the special educational needs assessment process and parental confidence. In this document the voice and engagement of children and young people with special educational needs were also raised: 'We need to take account of the views of children and young people and use their feedback to inform the development of schools and services' (DCSF, 2009a: 5.4, 70).

In response to the Lamb Inquiry's findings, the Children and Families Act 2014 and the current *SEN and Disability Code of Practice: 0 to 25 Years* (DfE and DoH, 2015) clearly identify the changes made from the 2001 SEN Code of Practice. The SEND Code of Practice says: 'There is a clearer focus on the participation of children and young people and parents in decision-making at individual and strategic levels' (DfE and DoH, 2015: 14). This is further reinforced in the first two principles which local authorities must have regard to. Although local authorities are given much of this responsibility, Section 1.4 states: 'Early years providers, schools and college should also take steps to ensure that young people . . . are actively supported in contributing to needs' assessments, developing and reviewing Education, Health and Care (EHC) plans' (DfE and DoH, 2015: 20).

At the end of Chapter 1, Section 1.40, a further directive is clearly delivered: 'All professionals working with families should look to enable children and young people to make choices for themselves from an early age.' As the post holder responsible for the SEN policy and ensuring national statutory

### Box 6.1 Hearing and responding to the voices of children and young people with special educational needs

**Practice ideas**

Collect and provide evidence of where and how children and young people with SEN participate actively in making decisions about:

1 their own progress and provision (provision maps, EHC plan reviews, target setting, marking feedback comments);
2 the resources and whole class/school provision for meeting their SEN;
3 establishment policies and systems;
4 what they would like to be more involved with/participate more in.

*Remember that historical and current evidence needs to be in your Ofsted file and also clearly tracked in the whole school development plans.*

1 You now know where and how you are already participating well with children and young people either at the individual teacher, SENCO or whole establishment level. To enable this good work to be built on carry out a whole establishment audit of how and where children or young people with SEN participate *actively* in decision-making and contributing to assessments, reports and reviews. Then identify where the gaps are, where the good practice is and the level of involvement. From this work you will be able to develop an action plan considering:
   i specific staff training and support needs;
   ii revisiting policies and processes, e.g. marking and feedback school protocols;
   iii evaluating the effectiveness of electronic and whole school tracking and assessment systems and the involvement of personnel due to time, place, costs;
   iv evaluate the terms of reference (effectiveness) of school forums, councils, timing of review meetings and children and young people's opportunities to put their ideas forward.

*Remember any review or new action needs to be introduced for all children and young people, but with particular thought given to the ways those of the community with SEN can also be included as full participants, e.g. school councils.*

guidance is followed, how can you as SENCO enhance your educational establishment's practice? Box 6.1 provides you with some questions to consider and will hopefully enable you to identify your establishment's starting point.

Although the ideas in Box 6.1 can be adapted easily to different settings and age groups the timeframe in which they can be introduced will vary dramatically, depending on staffing levels, staffing expertise and training, funding and resources. Thus, as SENCO, you must be realistic when and where you introduce new practices and processes to ensure that they are a success and positively received by all colleagues.

## 6.2 Parents and carers as partners

You might be surprised to know that even the original Code of Practice (DfE, 1994: 2:28: 12–13) included a paragraph about partnership with parents, emphasizing their role in a child's or young person's progress, stating:

> Professional help can seldom be wholly effective unless it builds upon parents' capacity to be involved and unless parents consider that professionals take account of what they say and treat their views and anxieties as intrinsically important.

Despite this statutory guidance, action for better and further improved parental partnership continued to be called for. Thus, the White Paper, *Excellence for All Children: Meeting Special Educational Needs* (DfES, 1997) was commissioned, and the findings set out the then government's strategy for ensuring parental involvement. This strategy highlighted three areas they felt the involvement of parents was vital. According to (DfES, 1997: 25–6), these were:

- for parents to have *choice* about the school their child or young person attends;
- for parents to have *entitlement* which was to be demonstrated through the improved monitoring of SEN provision and also improved confidence in what a school delivers for their child or young person;
- for parents to work in *partnership* with schools and Local Education Authorities; to share the knowledge they have to help schools make the right provisions for their child or young person.

It was hoped that this direction would lower both the number of SEN Tribunals and also requests for Statements of Special Educational Needs. However, the response by LEAs and schools was clearly not as robust as they wanted and in the revised SEN Code Practice (DfES, 2001a), a whole chapter focused on LEAs and schools working better with parents. In Section 2:2 (DfES, 2001a: 16), it stated: 'All parents of children with special educational needs should be treated as partners.' It also required all LEAs to put in place arrangements for parent partnerships services which would meet minimum standards of information, advice and support. The roles and responsibilities of schools were set out, stating that all staff 'have an important role in developing positive and constructive relationships with parents' (DfES, 2001a: 26) and that they should value the contribution of parents and recognize that this may require them to provide parents with both practical help and emotional support. It was also here that all maintained school were required (had to) to publish their SEN policy in a format that parents could understand. However, despite these statutory government interventions, there continued to be further guidance and legislation delivered about working in partnerships with parents towards the later years in the first decade of this century. Table 6.1 shows the ones which are important for SENCOs to be aware of. You will see Table 6.1 also illustrates the most significant aspects of parental partnership working and how they have influenced the most recent changes in special educational needs policy and practice.

**Table 6.1** Government materials promoting partnership with parents (2007–2010)

| *Details* | *Publisher and date of publication* | *Promotes partnership with parents* |
|---|---|---|
| *Every Parent Matters* | DfES, 2007b | This document stresses the importance of understanding how family circumstances and their expectations can impact on children and young people's behaviour and learning in school. It also identified the importance of fathers' involvement in children achieving positive outcomes. |
| *The Children's Plan: Two Years On: A Progress Report* | DCSF, 2009b | This emphasizes the important role of the school in working with parents to help their children achieve and reach their potential. It also highlights the importance of early intervention and working together. |
| *The Lamb Inquiry* | DCSF, 2009a | This document asked parents whether they had confidence in the SEN system of assessment. It made 51 recommendations, many of which focus on engaging with and the needs of parents (e.g. Recommendations 3, 4, 8, 16). Chapter 3 (Recommendations 13–20) is called 'a stronger voice for parents' and recommendations here all focus on working with parents. It proposed, for example, that Pupil Referral Units (PRU) should have to publish a SEN Policy, that there should be an advice line for parents with children with SEN and that Partnership with Parents should be re-launched to provide parents with high quality and expert advice. |
| *Achievement for All: Guidance for Schools* | DCSF, 2009c | One of this guidance's three key aims was to improve the engagement of parents of children and young people with SEND with their schools. It is now a charity supporting schools to implement the 'Achievement for All' framework: http://afaeducation.org/ (accessed 23 February 2016) |
| *Improving Parental Confidence in the Special Educational Needs System: An Implementation Plan* | DCSF, 2010c | One of the four key elements of this document stated that parents and carers needed to be heard, e.g. the implementation of a phone line. This plan also said that they would make schools more accountable for the SEN provision they offered, that they would help schools to manage bullying related to SEN/disability. |

From this information you will be able to see how and why parents are now considered key in all our work in early years provision, schools and especially in our work with children and young people with special educational needs. This is also explicit within the three special educational needs (and disabilities) Codes of

Practice. In the original Code of Practice (DfE, 1994), there was only a paragraph about working with parents, but a whole chapter in the revised SEN Code of Practice (DfES, 2001a) was devoted to this topic.

Now in the current Code of Practice parents are key members in its underpinning principles. Local authorities must have regard to the following:

- the views, wishes and feelings of the child or young person, and the child's parents;
- the importance of the child or young person, and the child's parents, participating as fully as possible in decisions, and being provided with the information and support necessary to enable participation in those decisions;
- the need to support the child or young person, and the child's parents, in order to facilitate the development of the child or young person.

(DfE and DoH, 2015: 1.1:19)

And early years provisions, schools and colleges should also ensure the learning of children and young people with special educational needs is informed by parental views and knowledge.

There is also an interesting emphasis placed in the SEND Code of Practice on preparing young people for adulthood and independence. It positively encourages and promotes the voice of the young person above that of the parent/carer beyond the age of 16. However, the SEND Code of Practice (DfE and DoH, 2015: 8.13: 126) still states that even when young people turn 16, parents and other family members will most likely 'remain closely involved in the great majority of cases', but only with the young person's agreement.

It also says that for a young person with special educational needs under 18, schools and colleges should 'continue to involve parents or family members in discussions about the young person's studies where that is their usual policy' (DfE and DoH, 2015: 8.17: 127).

For the SENCO looking to provide outstanding support, care and education for all children and young people with special educational needs, it is therefore crucial to ensure parental engagement and participation, and not just involvement, are embedded throughout the whole establishment. Once again, this is not something the SENCO is in charge of but an aspect of the roles and responsibilities of all teachers, the Senior Leadership Team (SLT) and governors or trustees. Nevertheless, it is the SENCO who will need to ensure the best practices are in place for the children and young people with special educational needs.

The following factors are important to remember when undertaking development in this area, when working with the majority of parents/carers:

- Parents/carers have a lot of valuable information, understanding and knowledge about a child or young person's special educational needs.
- Parents/carers want to be involved in their son's or daughter's education.
- Parents/carers have an important role to play in encouraging, motivating and supporting their children and young people with their learning.

### Case study 6.1 Seeing red

A Year 7 student with Autism Spectrum Disorder (ASD) joined a new secondary school. The SENCO and teachers had worked hard to provide a personalized map of provision. All was going well except for all science lessons. The student liked the subject, the teacher and his peers, and even targeted observations could not identify why as soon as he entered the science lab he became distressed and started throwing the seats around and refused to sit down.

The science teacher and the SENCO consulted the student's parents, as he was unable to articulate or use visual supports to provide them with a reason. The science teacher took the parents to his classroom and within a minute the parents had solved the problem. The student would not sit on, use or eat anything that was red. The seats were red!

### Case study 6.2 Video Interaction Guidance

In nursery it was becoming very clear to the teacher that some of the parents of children with a speech, language and communication need (SLCN) were finding it hard to know how to communicate and play effectively with them. The nursery teacher and nursery nurses had held 1:1 parent meetings and whole group workshops for all parents, providing suggestions to help develop these skills. An opportunity meant that a number of nursery parents could receive a course of Video Interaction Guidance (VIG) sessions with trained guiders focused on communication. These sessions can be quite intense and require commitment and trust in the professionals by the parents. With encouragement and support from the nursery staff, the SLT and the guiders, the parents completed the course. Despite the high level of commitment required, at the end, some of the parents identified that they would like to see VIG being offered to help parents learn how to help their child read in Years 1–3 and in the secondary years to help with relationships. See www.videointeractionguidance.net

### Case study 6.3 Parental involvement

At a 1:1 provision map review meeting with a parent and child who was on the SEN register for literacy needs, the SENCO asked the parent to spend some time every evening reading with her child. The parent said that she wanted to do this to help, but didn't know how she could do this regularly because her household is very busy in the evening and she had two younger children to look after as well. At the time the school was implementing the Achievement for All programme, including Structured Conversations and the SENCO and class teacher invited this parent to become part of this. With good communication and support from the SENCO for the teacher, a plan of how reading practice time could be included in their evening schedule was agreed and acted upon. The parent enjoyed being so involved in her child's development and the child's reading improved brilliantly. See https://afaeducation.org

**Table 6.2** Working in partnership with parents/carers whose children have special educational needs

1 COMMUNICATION:
- How do you as SENCO communicate with parents? Is this enough and is it effective? Why/why not?
- How do all staff communicate with parents?
- What do you communicate to parents? Is it positive as well as not so positive news?
- Do you have protocols or methods of recording meetings and conversations which everyone can access (if need be, remembering confidentiality)?

2 POLICIES:
- Is the SEN Information Report easily accessible for parents?
- Is the SEN Policy easy to read for parents, e.g. no jargon?
- Is a parent given a copy of the SEN policy when their child is placed on the SEN register and is it discussed at this point?
- Is consideration given to how parents who do not have English as their first language or cannot read find out about what the school provides?
- Does your policy ensure that parents know where to go for additional help or information?
- Is it on display in the school as well as on the website?
- Are staff regularly encouraged to engage with the SEN policy?
- Have all governors or trustees a good understanding of the SEN policy?

3 PAPERWORK:
- Do you have sample letters written and saved on disks for easy access for parents? Do you email them to parents as well as give them a paper copy?
- Do they all have a place for the date to be written (including the YEAR)?
- Are parents/carers and staff required to sign agreements or actions at the end of meetings with dates for completion noted? (This could also include the children and young people.)
- Do you have checklists which give you all the questions you need to ask when you attend specific meetings, e.g. preparing for an EHC plan?
- Do you have different information sheets detailing how different needs can impact on a child's or young person's learning?

4 TIME: When as a school do you offer parents' meetings?
- Do you have an open door policy or not?
- Do you have a surgery for parents/carers?
- Have you considered when shift workers and others can make meetings at school?
- When do you put workshops on or coffee 'mornings'? Are these the best time for parents?
- Also where do you offer support?

5 SUPPORT/TRAINING:
- Do you offer support groups or training sessions for parents? If so, when do you do this? Is it convenient for them? Do you provide a crèche or childcare?
- Parenting groups?
- Parent forums?
- Meet another professional time?
- Do you open your doors to other professionals wanting to work with families?

**Table 6.2** (continued)

6 STAFF CONFIDENCE:
- Do you as a school and specifically as the SENCO support staff through training, working alongside and modelling to work confidently with parents/carers?
- Do you plan training sessions across the year about having conversations with parents with children or young people with special educational needs?
- Do you help teachers think about how they can provide children or young people with homework parents can help them with, e.g. information for parents?

7 GOVERNORS:
- Do you provide at least termly updates to the SEN governor about any difficulties or positives working with parents/carers?
- Do governors or trustees attend parent forums or councils?
- Do they discuss changes to the SEN policy with parents/carers?

8 PARTICIPATION:
- How do you show parents/carers that their view matters and is important?
- How do parents participate in your establishment's activities and decision-making?
- How much do you value parental participation?
- Do you encourage parents to join the local authority Parent Carer Forums (DfE and DoH, 2015: 1.13: 22)?

9 TRUST:
- This is vital. How do you ensure parents can trust you and the teachers they work with? What does this enable you to achieve?
- Who in your establishment is best at fostering trust? Who? Which age group? How?

These three key factors and the case studies illustrate how the SENCO and all other staff can work effectively and in partnership with parents with children and young people with special educational needs. These examples do not include working with parents who have a child who have high-level needs, perhaps even requiring an assessment for an Education, Health and Care (EHC) plan, but they do show how by being open, willing to listen and learn, and by offering to provide additional support, parents can support their children's learning.

At this point I would like you to reflect on how you as a SENCO and all staff in the school particularly work with parents/carers with children and young people with special educational needs. Table 6.2 offers some prompts to help you see where good practice is already secure and where further work needs to be undertaken. Remember you do not have to be *the* professional who makes the changes, but you can be the one to lead the change and to embed it into practices and policies.

This reflection will help you add actions to your plan for the year(s). You will also begin to see how this way of working interweaves with other stakeholder partnerships, enabling you and all involved to ensure the child or young person's needs are always at the centre of discussions rather than focusing on how you are going to develop trust or share responsibilities.

## 6.3 Working with other professionals

This is without doubt I believe one of the most essential roles of the SENCO and one which requires hard work and a non-judgemental approach. With the increasing and complex needs of children and young people with special educational needs within our environments, SENCOs need to ensure they understand and can confidently liaise with a wide range of partners with different workforce protocols and requirements. With this expertise you can help guide and direct other staff members including the SLT (Senior Leadership Team) to understand why specific tasks or engagement are not possible for specific professionals. It is also I suggest one of the most exciting and rewarding aspects of the role. Many of my really important and long-term professional relationships are with colleagues from other professions. These were achieved through showing respect, understanding and transparency, enabling trust and a willingness to work as co-operatively as possible to grow. Working in this way can also in some cases be frustrating and difficult, especially in such a period of extreme change as is currently taking place in England, but when a plan comes together for a child or young person, the outcomes can be so positive and the value in working in this way becomes vividly clear.

First, therefore, let's look at what professional bodies are currently expected to be responsible for. Within the current SEND Code of Practice (DfE and DoH, 2015: 3.70: 56–7) the key roles and responsibilities of bodies involved in joint commissioning are set out for you. In this summary you will note that local authorities have the responsibility to 'lead integration' while all health and social care bodies must or are expected to co-operate with others, including the local authority. There is one area, however, where the government requires local authorities to provide a co-ordinated approach. Local authorities are now responsible for the effective co-ordination of the assessment and development process for an EHC plan (DfE and DoH, 2015: 9.30: 149–50). Finally, where the principles underpinning the SEND Code of Practice (DfE and DoH, 2015: 1.2: 19) are described, it states that they are designed to support: 'collaboration between education, health and social care services to provide support'. Why this change of terminology and what does this mean for practice and how SENCOs can expect children and young people to receive support and provision?

Joint working or joint commissioning means that more than one agency must work together with either a family, child, budget or project. It is also appropriate to say that the manner in which professionals and agencies or bodies work together should not be viewed as static, but as a process which moves across 'integrated partnership approaches' on a continuum 'from co-operation to integration (Frost, 2005; Stone and Rixon, 2008)' (Davis, 2011: 14). The four terms in regular use currently are 'co-operation', 'collaboration', 'co-ordination' and 'integration'. Table 6.3 defines these terms and how they may influence the evolution of a service or joint working.

Much of the requirements of the SEND Code of Practice (DfE and DoH, 2015) I suggest are encouraging our working practices to develop in the manner Davis (2011: 16) describes as '*Process-based* integrated working'. This way of working 'involves organised mergers, whole systems approaches, service level agreements, local flexibility, teamwork, joint learning and/or liaison' (Davis, 2011: 16). Davis continues to say that, 'At the centre of this shift is the notion that there is something extra gained from building strong trustful professional relationships' (Davis, 2011: 16).

**Table 6.3** Definitions of joined up working approaches

| *Term* | *Definition* |
|---|---|
| Co-operation | Information sharing between agencies working with children. It requires agencies to work across and outside of their traditional boundaries (Anning et al., 2006), but they continue to work separately and independently. |
| Collaboration | Collaboration is difficult to put into everyday practice. For collaboration to take place, services plan together (joint planning). They will aim to avoid duplicating services and to provide individual children or young people with all the services they require. This way of working can actually enable released resources from the joint planning to fill gaps in provision. Sometimes joint working will develop out of joint planning and in these circumstances agencies might work alongside each other or separately (but in a planned way). Collaboration, however, does not mean the agencies will share service or provision goals. |
| Co-ordination | Co-ordination is much more systematic than collaboration. When services are co-ordinated, it means that different agencies not only plan and work together, but take account of each other's aims, values, finances and expectations. |
| Integration | Full integration occurs when services are amalgamated – when different agencies or services become one, e.g. Early Years' Services. |

**Table 6.4** A service directory

| *Service or agency* | *Contact's name* | *Contact's details* | *Services available* | *Additional notes* |
|---|---|---|---|---|
| | | | | |

**Practice question**

With this understanding in mind, how can you ensure that as SENCO you are accessing support from the most appropriate agency or professional services and develop an appropriate and effective working partnership?

### The SENCO role in partnership working

Although promoted for a number of years, constructing a directory of agencies, services and partners would still be the most helpful first step for a SENCO (Table 6.4). With such a list names, emails and numbers can be quickly updated and shared across your setting. It is also very helpful to include a column with little extra pieces of information about when and how each agency, service or even individual professional works. Will you get a quick response if you email or do you need to ring at a certain time on a specific day? This is all vital information which should be on your setting's shared drive or in a secure place which can be accessed by senior leaders.

When working with other professionals, it is important to be clear about your role and also about the time and amount of work you will be expected to undertake within each partnership. You must also be very certain that each partnership is providing the outcomes you expect for the children or young people you work with, as if it does not, why invest your time and energy? This should be much easier as the Local Offer become more comprehensive.

The SEND Code of Practice (DfE and DoH, 2015: 59–60) clearly states that local authorities must publish a Local Offer and that this should:

- provide clear, comprehensive, accessible and up-to-date information about the available provision and how to access it, and
- make provision more responsive to local needs and aspirations by directly involving disabled children and those with SEN and their parents, and disabled young people and those with SEN, and service providers in its development and review.

Therefore, it is vital to keep both quantitative and qualitative data about the impact and service each partner provides. Such a way of working can also be beneficial when reviewing children's or young people's progress and achievement. Are all agencies or services fulfilling their responsibilities and their service level agreements? In order to challenge this appropriately you will need evidence to clearly demonstrate how things need to improve. This is where templates where feedback or information can be quickly written are invaluable. With a calendar-type approach this collection of notes and information can provide a very useful specific and overall picture of how successful working with a partner is.

Of course partnerships might also involve staff training or specialist resources, but the same approach will be necessary to ensure you are providing the best possible service you can to the provision, school or college and of course the children, young people and families.

### Chairing a multi-professional meeting

Being able to hold and chair a meeting, and especially a multi-professional one needs careful planning and preparation. Much of the work can actually be carried out by a SEN administrator or assistant, but you as SENCO need to be able to be confident that all important aspects have been considered prior to the start of the meeting.

Always consider:

- the date of the meeting:
  - has it been agreed and confirmed by all members of the meeting?
  - how is this followed up? By whom? Perhaps a written report or telephone conferencing can be arranged to ensure the meeting is successful.
  - was the invitation to a parent sent out in good time and followed up by a phone call or face-to-face conversation?
  - was a reminder sent to the parent/carer via text/phone on the day or the previous day?

- the timing of the meeting:
  - is it too near the end of the day when children need to be collected or traffic jams need to be avoided?
- the room and layout;
  - is it private, warm and welcoming?
- does the agenda take account of participants' anxieties and each voice?
  - why leave the contribution from the parent until last?
- are all staff and other stakeholders able to attend?
  - if not, can you make the decisions you need to?

Also always remember:

- have tissues available;
- have water or other refreshments available;
- have a minute taker (preferably a SEN administrator or assistant);
- have information or legislation you might need to refer to, easily to hand;
- have a mobile phone available to ask for assistance or information;
- ensure parking has been organized;
- ensure visitor badges are readily available;
- have a box of toys and books if children are present;
- have an appropriate room if a member of the meeting has a sensory difficulty;
- ensure there are toilets nearby.

Chairing a meeting can be frightening, especially when it is the first time or a very difficult case. This is when planning and preparation can really support you. Much of the elements above can be produced on a checklist for the SEN administrator or assistant to complete. This allows you as SENCO to focus on the content

**Box 6.2 Key aspects of chairing a successful meeting**

1. Ensure everyone is in agreement with the agenda prior to the meeting.
2. Set a timeframe for the meeting and stick to it. Two hours means two hours.
3. Set out at the beginning what needs to be achieved by the end of the meeting and remain focused on achieving these outcomes.
4. Make everyone feel comfortable, valued and listened to. Give time for introductions.
5. Make it clear when and how refreshments will be available.
6. Set clear boundaries stating that all participants need to speak through the Chair. In this way you can ensure all participants get a chance to share their information and knowledge and have their views heard.
7. Have all the information about the child or agency you need available in front of you and copies required for sharing in readiness.
8. Have the minute taker positioned next to you, the Chair.
9. Make sure the meeting is well paced and flows well, without feeling rushed.
10. Remain positive and engaged throughout.

and procedure of the actual meeting. Following the 10 steps in Box 6.2 can help you run a successful professional meeting where everyone feels heard and valued and where outcomes are achieved within an expected timeframe.

### Core principles of working with others

#### Practice suggestions

As a SENCO, consider what the core principles of working together for you are. Remember though that partnership working means just that and therefore you should not and actually must not be expected to carry out all the actions or have the responsibility for all the outcomes for a child or young person with special educational needs.

The following may help:

- Respect each partner.
- Build trusting and open professional relationships.
- Develop your own knowledge and understanding of other professionals' roles and responsibilities.
- Achieve a common understanding of the language used by all partners.
- Achieve a common understanding of each other's aims.
- Achieve a common understanding of required outcomes for the children or young people with special educational needs.

## 6.4 Working with governors, volunteers and the wider community

### Governing bodies

The partners to be discussed here are ones I suggest, can, for the majority of SENCOs, be the most difficult to establish and maintain. Governors of maintained schools (including academies and free schools) have responsibilities to ensure their schools have employed a qualified teacher as a SENCO (DfE and DoH, 2015). This guidance also says that there should 'be a member of the governing body or a sub-committee with specific oversight of the school's arrangements for SEN and disability' (DfE and DoH, 2015: 6.3: 92). However, it is not always easy for SENCOs to work regularly with a governor to help promote and enhance SEN strategic development and provision which will lead to improved outcomes.

Within the roles of the SENCO, the SEND Code of Practice (DfE and DoH, 2015: 6.87: 108) also tries to encourage governor involvement with the SENCO, and children and young people with special educational needs, by saying that the SENCO 'has an important role to play with the headteacher and governing body in determining the strategic development of the SEN policy and provision in the school' (DfE and DoH, 2015). This is not feasible, however, if the SENCO is not a member of the senior leadership. To try to help, local authorities have provided guidance to governors about their role in working with the SENCO and with responsibility for SEN provision. The School Governor website: https://school-governors.thekeysupport.com/the-governing-body/roles-on-the-governing-body/link-governors/the-role-of-the-sen-governor#section-1 (accessed 23 February 2016) provides a case study example that shows how a SEN governor can support the SENCO and SEN work within their establishment.

### Case study 6.4 Governors' role

The London Borough of Barking and Dagenham has guidance for its schools on the role of a governor with responsibility for SEN provision.

The guidance says that the role of an SEN governor includes:

- helping to raise awareness of SEND issues at governing body meetings;
- ensuring that the school's notional SEN budget is appropriately allocated to support pupils with SEN;
- giving up-to-date information to the governing body on the quality and effectiveness of SEN and disability provision within the school
- helping to review the school's policy on provision for pupils with SEN;
- assuring the governing body that the school website publishes the school's SEN offer.

https://www.lbbd.gov.uk/wp-content/uploads/2014/12/School-Governors-SEN-and-Inclusion-Governor-job-description.pdf (accessed 23 February 2016)

With the requirement for governing bodies to write and publicly share an SEN information report on their establishment's website (applicable to maintained nursery schools, maintained schools and academies) as detailed in the new SEND Code of Practice (DfE and DoH, 2015: 6.79: 106–7), SENCOs need to provide the governing bodies with links to relevant national legislation and a clear action plan of how the nursery or school (and hopefully colleges) are ensuring they meet the government's statutory requirements.

### Practice questions

- Using all of the information and strategies gained throughout this book so far, think about what aspects of the SEN information report you can easily explain and evidence to your governing body. What do you still need to implement or enhance?
- How well does the SEN information report link to the Local Offer?
- Have you developed your own SEN information report using the details in the SEND Code of Practice or the one your local authority has suggested?
- How often are you asked to provide a report or speak with the governors or via the SEN governor?
- How often do you meet your SEN governor?

- Do you have an annual programme in place to support and inform the SEN governor about the support and progress of the children and young people with special educational needs?

Remember this SEN information report must be updated regularly and at least annually, and it should not include jargon or SEN-specific language. To help with this I suggest that you ask your parent forum or parent council and the pupil/student council to work through both the SEN policy and the SEN information report with you.

The Annual Programme for a SEN governor could include:

- a learning SEN walk around the school;
- tracking anonymized data for pupils/students on the SEN register with and without an EHC plan or a statement of special educational needs;
- a discussion about the establishment's data for children with special educational needs in comparison to all its other pupils/students, and compared to local and national data;
- an understanding of the resources and interventions available to use with children and young people with special educational needs – are more required? This will clearly be included with the wider discussion about funding for SEN support (the notional SEN budget which is not ring-fenced). This could also include discussions about how other targeted resources such as pupil premium could best be used.
- an understanding of how the establishment supports and achieves the appropriate outcomes for children and young people with different needs through its high quality teaching, targeted intervention and specialist provision;
- an overview of the training needs of staff;
- a meeting with parents/carers of children or young people with special educational needs to identify any areas where the provision, school or college could improve. This could be also carried out with the children or young people themselves.
- paperwork and other parent information can be reviewed together in preparation for the whole governing body's agreement;
- a discussion about your role as SENCO.

This is not of course an exclusive list, but hopefully it will help you identify specific areas where you feel focus is required to move the strategic development of SEN forward.

#### Volunteers

During these economically difficult times, do not forget to identify and then work effectively with local or national charities and volunteers. When you start exploring your local areas and engage with the Local Offer, I suspect you will find one or two charities or groups of volunteers you feel would benefit the children or young people in your establishment. Your local library or book clubs might also be able to provide support with resources or time, as could your local university. Be creative in locating new opportunities and always think about the children and young people's development into adulthood, whatever their age.

Do not forget to ensure all necessary safeguarding checks and written parental permissions (and the children's or young people's consent) are gained prior to commencing programmes such as 1:1 reading time with a regular volunteer.

### The community

Why not try to involve the community in supporting different opportunities for children and young people with special educational needs. This could be a project about raising money for a local or international charity or about helping to decorate the local youth club. In this way the children and young people with special educational needs are learning how to engage and socialize in the wider community.

Working together can be very time-consuming and complex and it can be in many different forms. However, partnership working can improve the outcomes for children and young people with special educational needs through co-ordinated approaches which focus on ensuring the child's needs are kept central to all provision and intervention.

## What does this mean for the SENCO?

- *Take time to review and reflect on the manner in which you work with other agencies and services. How effective are your partnerships? How can you improve them?*
- *Do not underestimate the complexity of joined-up working.*
- *Make sure you understand the remit of each partner you are working with.*
- *See if there is any possibility of merging paperwork structures so that it can save you all time and duplication.*
- *Ensure that you are all clear about how you are trying to work together. Reflect on the language used in this chapter to help you make decisions.*
- *Doing this will help you be more realistic about what can be achieved and with whom.*

## Direct Links to the SEND Code of Practice

- vi There is a clearer focus on the participation of children and young people and parents in decision-making at individual and strategic levels.
- vi It includes guidance on the joint planning and commissioning of services to ensure close co-operation between education, health and social care.
- 1.3 Local authorities must ensure that children, their parents and young people are involved in discussions and decisions about their individual support and about local provision.
- 1.4 Early years providers, schools and colleges should also take steps to ensure that young people and parents are actively supported in contributing to needs assessments, developing and reviewing Education, Health and Care (EHC) plans.

- 1.9 Local authorities must ensure that children, young people and parents are provided with the information, advice and support necessary to enable them to participate in discussions and decisions about their support.
- 1.22 If children and young people with SEN or disabilities are to achieve their ambitions and the best possible educational and other outcomes, including getting a job and living as independently as possible, local education, health and social care services should work together to ensure they get the right support.
- 9.36 Joint working between local authorities and CCGs (Clinical Commissioning Groups) in the development of an EHC plan supports the provision of effective services for children and young people with SEN.

# 7 A SENCO calendar

This final chapter will draw together points discussed throughout this book showing how this simple approach can be so helpful when you begin to write your SEN three-year strategic plan. It will emphasize the importance of being realistic about what you can achieve. To help you consider this carefully, factors such as available time, staffing, level of need and team work will be used to illustrate how these can influence timescales and pace of change. The management of expectations and your own well-being will be introduced in an attempt to help you develop ways of working which enable you to sustain your role as a SENCO while still having a positive work–life balance.

## 7.1 Well-being

Although this is not an issue which is relevant only to SENCOs, it is one which is important for you to be aware of when you are planning your calendar. To be able to remain effective for colleagues and to the children or young people you are working with, you need to ensure that you take care of yourself. So often we think that we are strong, resilient and can weather any storm, but over a long period of time, if we neglect to take care of ourselves and try always to say 'yes', our balanced view, the ability to be strategic and effective will be negatively impacted upon. Read the following practice questions and answer them honestly.

**Practice questions**

- How much regular teaching do you do?
- How frequently are you asked to step in to teach a class or group at the last moment?
- When do you listen to or take concerns from colleagues?
- When do you have the 'do not disturb' sign on your door to enable you to complete some paperwork during the nursery/school/college day? Is this respected by colleagues? If not, think why this might be the case.
- How much work do you take home to complete over the course of a week?
- Do you ensure that confidential information remains at work?
- What outside work activities do you do on a weekly basis?
- How well do you think you eat or exercise?
- Who do you have to talk to confidentially to ensure that you emotionally process stressful situations you have experienced?

Now take a look at how you organize your diary each week. You will clearly have important regular internal and external meetings which must be attended. Your teaching commitment must also be immediately put in your weekly planner. Look at the last four weeks and all the activities you have carried out during the day. Alongside this, write down what work you have completed during evenings and weekends. What does this tell you about how you are managing your workload?

- List the tasks you have completed under headings such as:
  - Teaching
  - Meeting parents or others
  - Statutory meetings
  - External meetings
  - Professional CPD and support, e.g. SENCO network meetings
  - Progress review meetings
  - Co-ordinating provision
  - Report and document writing
  - INSET or training
  - Consultations with colleagues
  - Completing assessments or observations
  - Performance management or managerial tasks
  - Strategic planning
- Now group similar tasks together and then write how many hours you have spent on each: (1) during the working day; and (2) outside of the normal working day. Here is a sample of what you might include (Table 7.1).

What do you notice? How much of your time are you spending teaching, managing and leading? Is this appropriately balanced considering the needs of the children or young people with special educational needs in your establishment? By carrying out this review of your working practices, you will be able to see if any areas need reviewing and perhaps even how improvements to your practice might be achieved. There are of course days when a significant event occurs and your 'to do' list gets only added to. But having periods of time blocked off for

**Table 7.1** Task organization

| *Group A Meetings* | *Group B Teaching* | *Group C Performance/CPD* | *Group D SENCO/ Assessment work* |
|---|---|---|---|
| 1. Statutory<br>2. Professional<br>3. Progress Review<br>4. Parental<br>5. Colleagues<br>6. Staff<br>7. Local Authority<br>8. SENCO networks | Monday – 9–12<br>Wednesday – 1–4<br>Thursday – all day | 1. INSET (whole staff)<br>2. Teaching Assistants 1:1<br>3. Consultations with staff<br>4. Lesson observations | 1. Observations<br>2. Assessments<br>3. Report writing<br>4. Request for high needs funding<br>5. Audit of resources<br>6. Reviewing provision maps |
| Time: | Time: | Time: | Time: |

specific tasks, such as report writing and specific staff or parental 'open door' times, will help you to manage those 'Can I just have a quick word?' times more efficiently. It will give you 'permission' to sit and write at work, instead of always leaving the writing tasks for after work at home in your family time. Also a review of your referral paperwork and what must be completed prior to asking you for assistance could also be helpful. Be critical, be objective and be firm in sticking to decisions which you make (in collaboration with the other senior leaders) to protect yourself in the long term and also provide clear guidance for colleagues.

When you have looked at this and apportioned your workload to various time periods, it will also support you, if it is a problem for you, to say to colleagues, 'I really cannot do XXX or YYY today because I have these deadlines for the completion of this work.' As we work more and more in collaboration with other professionals providing commissioned pieces of work, meeting deadlines and completing targets to achieve outcomes are going to become vital. Thus, working one or two evenings a week (into the night often!) could easily become every evening if you are not careful, always leaving the reports and document writing to later.

Be *realistic* about what you can achieve with the resources and time you have available. If your establishment provides four hours a week for you to carry out the SENCO role, the timeframe in which actions are going to be achieved is going to be very different to those who are SENCOs full-time. Completing this weekly work plan will show you where you may be able to delegate certain tasks, to other colleagues, for example, or where you need to further develop the use of your intranet system (if you have one) so that it aids more effective communication and information sharing. This is where thinking strategically can help you manage the day-to-day roles and responsibilities of your SENCO role. Always consider asking the question 'Does it have to be me who completes this action or does another colleague or external specialist have the skills and capacity?' I suggest that 'Yes' will only be the answer some of the time.

This detailed review and reflection of your daily working pattern will contribute to your three-year strategic planning, ensuring that you are realistic and also confident about who and how both whole establishment and specific SEN tasks can be developed and enhanced.

## 7.2 Time for change

Throughout this whole manual it has been made very clear that the role of the SENCO is not just about managing and co-ordinating, but about leadership as well. The role requires SENCOs not only to be leaders with vision and a mission, but also leaders who can understand the importance of business and financial planning, and implementation acumen.

With growing economic uncertainty and pressure on the public purse, the speed of change cannot continue to 'take time' if children and young people with special educational needs, as well as all others, are going to be able to have access to high quality education. As a SENCO, therefore, the manner in which you manage the new national and local requirements and provision systems will be really

**Table 7.2** The SEN Development/Action Plan

| *Specific objectives* | *Whole establishment actions* | *Year/Group/Department Actions* | *Who and when by?* | *Review of progress* |
|---|---|---|---|---|
| To develop a more outcomes-focused approach re: SEND practice | Staff to be actively focused on provision driven by outcomes. Targets need to be SMART and linked to areas of special educational needs | Personalized plans or provision maps with costings and evidence of effectiveness for outcomes | All staff<br>Terms 3 and 4 | Achieved<br>Term 4 |
| | EVIDENCE: Development of work achieved in progress review/department meetings | EVIDENCE: All children's or young people's profiles to be presented electronically in this way | | |
| To audit, provide and more effectively evaluate the interventions on offer | Audit of all interventions on offer across the establishment, detailing where they are located and the purpose. Identify gaps and levels of evaluation of intervention effectiveness measured | All this information to be shared and located on intranet for all staff to use. Identify any further needs through review meetings and staff meetings | SENCO/all other Senior Leaders/ all staff<br>Term 3 | SENCO completed audit and gaps identified. Further work with staff required<br>Term 3 |
| | EVIDENCE: Audit completed with gaps in provision located and intervention effectiveness evidenced | EVIDENCE: Intervention sheets and provision maps will all have these interventions (universal, targeted and specialist) on | | |
| To communicate and liaise more effectively with feeder provision/ schools/ SENCO to support smoother transitions | Develop opportunities for SENCOs, Year leaders and teachers to spend time pre- and post-transition time. For SENCO to spend time with feeder establishment SENCOs and children or young people with SEN prior to transition<br>Develop Transition Environmental Action Plan<br>EVIDENCE: SENCO more involved in transition planning and preparation for children or young people with SEN | All aware of importance of transitions and to look at their own welcoming and induction processes and activities for those with special educational needs<br>EVIDENCE: All children or young people tell and show SENCO/ teachers/parents that the transition process (internal or external) is working well | On-going throughout year with particular focus in Terms 4, 5 ,6 and 1<br>SENCO/other Senior Leaders all staff/ children/young people | Limited movement – further work required to enable effective SENCO input |

important if inclusive practices are not only going to be able to continue, but to grow and extend their tentacles throughout your whole educational establishment.

## 7.3 A calendar fit for purpose

Using many of the suggestions and ideas found throughout this book start to populate your SENCO calendar for the new term or new academic year. Put in the 'cannot be moved' activities first and then using the provision/school/college development plan or calendar of events begin to map your more specific SEN needs. You will not get this right first time, but it will, I suspect, immediately help you see why you need to protect certain periods of time during the year. Doing this with ready access to the whole establishment calendar will also enable you to see where events or meetings can be completed together. Appendix 3 provides a sample of what your annual calendar might look like. The example is very simplistic, but even this one begins to identify a couple of gaps where development or CPD work might be able to be comfortably included.

### Strategic planning (one or three years)

After completing an accurate 'calendar' of your roles and responsibilities (Appendix 3), you will begin to appreciate first of all what actions need to be taken and then how many can be positively achieved: (1) in line with the establishment's overall development plan; and (2) with the available time. Table 7.2 provides you with a skeleton outline of what your one- and three-year plan might include.

## 7.4 Final words

It is hoped that you are now confident and well enough informed to move forward in your role as SENCO, knowing how to balance and delegate the many administrative, managerial and leadership tasks you will be expected to fulfil. You will also understand the value of parental partnership and multi-professional working and always consider the well-being of your staff as well as the children and young people with special educational needs. Undoubtedly the SENCO role will continue to twist and turn as it evolves further, but the main role – ensuring children and young people with special educational needs receive the education they deserve and need – I am sure will never change. Keep being passionate, keep being an advocate and keeping believing in the journey which is inclusion.

### What does this mean for the SENCO?

- *If new to post, take time to review and reflect. Do not be tempted to rush in trying to solve multiple matters simultaneously.*
- *Carry out audits to provide you with the information you require before you can make evidence-based decisions.*
- *Work in collaboration with all other senior leaders or managers so that you can perhaps introduce or enhance new materials or methods of collecting*

*data which will be beneficial to children and young people with special educational needs as well as all others.*

- *Do not expect to solve all the changes required within a short period of time (e.g. one academic year).*
- *Identify a few quick 'wins' and one or two medium- and long-term developments and start with these. Obviously work with your Ofsted or any other inspection reports you have to help you select these.*

## Direct links to the SEND Code of Practice

- 5.60 Early Years providers should consider how best to use their resources to support the progress of children with SEN.
- 6.91 The school should ensure that the SENCO has sufficient time and resources to carry out these functions. This should include providing the SENCO with sufficient administrative support and time away from teaching to enable them to fulfil their responsibilities in a similar way to other important strategic roles within a school.
- 6.92 It may be appropriate for a number of smaller primary schools to share a SENCO employed to work across the individual schools, where they meet the other requirements set out in this chapter of the Code. Schools can consider this arrangement where it secures sufficient time away from teaching and sufficient administrative support to enable the SENCO to fulfil the role effectively for the total registered pupil population across all of the schools involved.

# Appendix 1

**Definition of special educational needs (SEN)**

xiii. A child or young person has SEN if they have a learning difficulty or disability which calls for special educational provision to be made for him or her.

xiv. A child of compulsory school age or a young person has a learning difficulty or disability if he or she:

- has a significantly greater difficulty in learning than the majority of others of the same age, or
- has a disability which prevents or hinders him or her from making use of facilities of a kind generally provided for others of the same age in mainstream schools or mainstream post-16 institutions.

xv. For children aged two or more, special educational provision is educational or training provision that is additional to or different from that made generally for other children or young people of the same age by mainstream schools, maintained nursery schools, mainstream post-16 institutions or by relevant early years providers. For a child under two years of age, special educational provision means educational provision of any kind.

xvi. A child under compulsory school age has special educational needs if he or she is likely to fall within the definition in paragraph xiv. above when they reach compulsory school age or would do so if special educational provision was not made for them (Section 20 Children and Families Act 2014).

Source: (DfE and DoH, 2015: 15–16)

# Appendix 2

### Definition of disabled children and young people

xviii. Many children and young people who have SEN may have a disability under the Equality Act 2010 – that is 'A physical or mental impairment which has a long-term and substantial adverse effect on their ability to carry out normal day-to-day activities.' This definition provides a relatively low threshold and includes more children than many realise: 'long-term' is defined as 'a year or more' and 'substantial' is defined as 'more than minor or trivial'. This definition includes sensory impairments such as those affecting sight or hearing, and long-term health conditions, such as asthma, diabetes, epilepsy, and cancer. Children and young people with such conditions do not necessarily have SEN, but there is a significant overlap between disabled children and young people and those with SEN. Where a disabled child or young person requires special educational provision, they will also be covered by the SEN definition.

xix. The Equality Act 2010 sets out the legal obligations that schools, early years providers, post-16 institutions, local authorities and others have towards disabled children and young people:

- they must not directly or indirectly discriminate against, harass or victimise disabled children and young people
- they must not discriminate for a reason arising in consequence of a child's or young person's disability.
- they must make reasonable adjustments, including the provision of auxiliary aids and services, to ensure that disabled children and young people are not at a substantial disadvantage compared with their peers. This duty is anticipatory – it requires thought to be given in advance to what disabled children and young people [and I would add here all adults working or visiting as well] might require and what adjustments might need to be made to prevent that disadvantage.
- Public bodies, including further education institutions, local authorities, maintained schools, maintained nursery schools, academies and free schools are covered by the public section equality duty and, when carrying out their functions, must have regard to the need to eliminate discrimination, promote equality of opportunity and foster good relations between disabled and non-disabled children and young people.

xx. Most providers must also make reasonable adjustments by making physical alterations. Schools and local authority education functions are not covered by this last duty, but they must publish accessibility plans (and local authorities, accessibility strategies) setting out how they plan to increase access for disabled pupils to the curriculum, the physical environment and to information [and again I would encourage for all adults as well].

Source: DfE and DoH (2015: 16–18)

# Appendix 3

## The SENCO calendar (termly)

| *Action* | *Term 1 Autumn Term* | *Term 2* | *Term 3 Spring Term* | *Term 4* | *Term 5 Summer Term* | *Term 6* |
|---|---|---|---|---|---|---|
| Progress Review Meetings | Activities | | | | | |
| SEN Policy Review | | | | | | |
| Performance Management | | | | | | |
| Transition Work | | | | | | |
| Provision Management | | | | | | |
| Parent/Carer SEN Review meetings | | | | | | |
| Assessments | | | | | | |
| SENCO Networking | Consultation | | | | | |
| Teaching | | | | | | |

Key:
Activities – light grey
Consultation – dark grey

# References


Anning, A., Cottrell, D., Frost, N., Green, J. and Robinson, M. (2006) *Developing Multiprofessional Teamwork for Integrated Children's Services*. Maidenhead: Open University Press.

Anthony, M. (2010) Business management and ensuring value for money. In S. Soan (ed.) *The SENCO Handbook* (2nd edn). London: Optimus Education.

Barton, L. (2010) The politics of education for all. In J. Rix, M. Nind, K. Sheehy, K. Simmons, K. Parry and R. Kimrai (eds) *Equality, Participation and Inclusion: Diverse Perspectives*. London: Routledge.

Bolman, L.G. and Deal, T.E. (1997) *Reframing Organisations: Artistry, Choice and Leadership*. San Francisco, CA: Jossey-Bass.

Booth, T. and Ainscow, M. (2002) *Index for Inclusion*. Bristol: CSIE.

Bush, T. (2003) *Educational Leadership and Management* (3rd edn). London: Sage.

Children and Families Act, 2014, London: Crown Copyright.

Cohen, L., Manion, L. and Morrison, K (2007) *Research Methods in Education* (6th edn). London: Routledge.

Cuban, L. (1988) *The Managerial Imperative and the Practice of Leadership in Schools*. Albany, NY: State University of New York Press.

David, T., Goouch, K. and Powell, S. (2011) Play and prescription: the influence of national developments in England. In M. Kernan and E. Singer (eds) *Peer Relationships in Early Childhood Education and Care*. London: Routledge, pp. 49–60.

Davis, J.M. (2011) *Integrated Children's Services*. London: Sage.

DCSF (2008) *The Bercow Report*. Annesley: DCSF. Available at: http://webarchive.nationalarchives.gov.uk/20130401151715/https:/www.education.gov.uk/publications/standard/publicationdetail/page1/DCSF-00632-2008 (accessed 23 February 2016).

DCSF (2009a) *The Lamb Inquiry: Special Educational Needs and Parental Confidence*. Annesley: DCSF. Available at: http://webarchive.nationalarchives.gov.uk/20100202100434/dcsf.gov.uk/lambinquiry/ (accessed 23 February 3016).

DCSF (2009b) *The Children's Plan: Two Years On: A Progress Report*. Annesley: DCSF.

DCSF (2009c) *Achievement for All: Guidance for Schools*. Annesley: DCSF.

DCSF (2010a) *The SALT Review*. Available at: http://webarchive.nationalarchives.gov.uk/tna/+/http:/www.dcsf.gov.uk/saltreview/downloads/SaltReportRevisedFinal.pdf (accessed 23 February 2016).

DCSF (2010b) *Breaking the Link between Special Educational Needs and Low Attainment*. Annesley: DCSF.

DCSF (2010c) *Improving Parental Confidence in the Special Educational Needs System: An Implementation Plan*. Annesley: DCSF.

DfE (1994) *Code of Practice on the Identification and Assessment of Special Educational Needs*. London: DfE.

DfE (2010) *The Importance of Teaching*. London: Crown Copyright.

DfE (2011) *Support and Aspiration: A New Approach to Special Educational Needs and Disability: A Consultation*. Norwich: TSO.

DfE (2015) *The Special Educational Needs and Disability Pathfinder Programme Evaluation Final Impact Research Report*. Available at: https://www.gov.uk/government/uploads/system/uploads/attachment_data/file/448157/RB471_SEND_pathfinder_programme_final_report_brief.pdf (accessed 9 February 2016).

DfE and DoH (2014) *Special Educational Needs Code of Practice: 0 to 25 Years*, London: DfE.

DfE and DoH (2015) *Special Educational Needs and Disability Code of Practice: 0 to 25 Years*. London: DfE. Available at: https://www.gov.uk/government/uploads/system/uploads/attachment_data/file/398815/SEND_Code_of_Practice_January_2015.pdf (accessed 9 March 2016).

DfES (1997) *Excellence for All Children: Meeting Special Educational Needs*. London: DfES.

DfES (2001a) *Special Educational Needs Code of Practice*. London: DfES.

DfES (2001b) *Inclusive Schooling*. Annesley: DfES.

DfES (2001c) *SEN Toolkit*. London: DfES.

DfES (2007a) *Making Good Progress*. London: DfES.

DfES (2007b) *Every Parent Matters*. Annesley: DfES.

Dimmock, C. (1999) Principals and school restructuring: conceptualising challenges as dilemmas. *Journal of Educational Administration*, 37(5): 441–62.

Education Act 1996. Section 316A, London: HMSO.

Ekins, A. (2012) *The Changing Face of Special Educational Needs*. London: Routledge.

Gray, C. and MacBlain, S. (2012) *Learning Theories in Childhood*. London: Sage.

HMSO (2008) *The Education (Special Educational Needs Coordinators) Regulations*. Available at: http://www.legislation.gov.uk/uksi/2008/2945/contents/made (accessed 23 February 2016).

HMSO (2009) *The Education (Special Educational Needs Coordinators (England) (Amended) Regulations* (2009 No. 1387). Available at: http://www.legislation.gov.uk/uksi/2009/1387/made (accessed 23 February 2016).

HM Treasury (2003) *Every Child Matters*. Norwich: TSO.

House of Commons Select Committee (2006) *Special Educational Needs: Third Report of Session 2005–2006*. London: TSO.

Humphrey, N. and Squires, G. (2011) *Achievement for All: National Evaluation*. Available at: https://www.gov.uk/government/uploads/system/uploads/attachment_data/file/193255/DFE-RB176.pdf (accessed 9 March 2016).

Kemmis, S. and McTaggart, R. (1992) *The Action Research Planner* (3rd edn). Geelong, Vic: Deakin University Press.

National College (2010) *A Special Achievement*. Nottingham: National College.

Norwich, B. (2002) Education, inclusion and individual differences. *British Journal of Educational Studies*, 50(4): 482–502.

Nussbaum, M.C. (2000) *Women and Human Development: The Capabilities Approach*. Cambridge: Cambridge University Press.

Ofsted (2010) *The Special Educational Needs and Disability Review: A Statement Is Not Enough*. Manchester: Crown Copyright.

Prout, A. (2005) *The Future of Childhood: Towards the Interdisciplinary Study of Children*. London: Falmer Press.

Rawls, J. (2001) *Justice as Fairness: A Restatement*. Cambridge, MA: Harvard University Press.

Redman, S., Downie, M., Rennison, R. and Batten, A. (2009) *Don't Write Me Off: Make the System Fair for People with Autism*. London: The National Autistic Society. Available at: www.autism.org.uk/~/media/nas/documents/dont%20write%20me%20off.ashx (accessed 14 September 2016).

Sen, A. (1980) Equality of what? In S. McMurrin (ed.) *The Tanner Lectures on Human Values*. Salt Lake City, UT: University of Utah Press.

Sen, A. (1992) *Inequality Reexamined*. Oxford: Clarendon Press.

Symes, W. and Humphrey, N. (2011) The deployment, training and teacher relationships of teaching assistants supporting pupils with autistic spectrum disorders (ASD) in mainstream secondary schools. *British Journal of Special Education*, 38(2): 57–64.

Terzi, L. (2010) *Justice and Equality in Education*. London: Continuum.

UNCRC (United Nations Convention on the Rights of the Child) (1989) Available at: www.unicef.org/crc/ (accessed 30 December 2015).

UNICEF, 1989: Articles 12 and 13. Available at: http://www.unicef.org/crc/files/Rights_overview.pdf (accessed 10 March 2016).

Warnock, M. (1978) *Warnock Report: Special Educational Needs, Report of the Committee of Enquiry into the Education of Handicapped Children and Young People*. London: HMSO.

Zelizer, V. (1994) *Pricing the Priceless Child: The Changing Social Value of Children*. Princeton, NJ: Princeton University Press.

# Index